Exquisite Little Knits

Exquisite Little Knits

Knitting with Luxurious Specialty Yarns

LAURIE KIMMELSTIEL • IRIS SCHREIER

A DIVISION OF STERLING PUBLISHING CO., INC. • NEW YORK

DEDICATION

Iris Schreier
For Elliot, Jason, and Owen

Laurie Kimmelstiel
For Fred, Jonah, Rebecca, and Jeremy

Editor: Suzanne J. E. Tourtillott

Art Directors: Dana Irwin (photography) and 828, Inc. (layout)

Photographer: Sandra Stambaugh

Cover Designer: Barbara Zaretsky

Illustrator: Olivier Rollin

Assistant Editor: Nathalie Mornu

Associate Art Director: Shannon Yokeley

Editorial Assistance: Delores Gosnell

Editorial Interns: Meghan McGuire, Amanda Wheeler

Special Photography: Kristi Pfeffer, contents and page 8; Sandra Stambaugh, page 6; Suzanne J. E. Tourtillott, pages 19–23

Notes About Suppliers:
Usually, the supplies you need for making the projects in Lark books can be found at your local craft supply store, discount mart, home improvement center, or retail shop relevant to the topic of the book. Occasionally, however, you may need to buy materials or tools from specialty suppliers. In order to provide you with the most up-to-date information, we have created a listing of suppliers on our Web site, which we update on a regular basis. Visit us at www.larkbooks.com, click on "Craft Supply Sources," and then click on the relevant topic. You will find numerous companies listed with their web address and/or mailing address and phone number.

Library of Congress Cataloging-in-Publication Data

Kimmelstiel, Laurie.
  Exquisite little knits : knitting with luxurious specialty yarns / Laurie Kimmelstiel, Iris Schreier.
    p. cm.
  Includes index.
  ISBN 1-57990-536-6 (hardcover)
  1. Knitting. I. Schreier, Iris. II. Title.
TT820.K4985 2004
746.43'2--dc22

2004005314

10 9 8 7 6 5 4 3 2

Published by Lark Books, a division of Sterling Publishing Co., Inc.
387 Park Avenue South, New York, N.Y. 10016

© 2004, Laurie Kimmelstiel and Iris Schreier

Distributed in Canada by Sterling Publishing, c/o Canadian Manda Group,
165 Dufferin Street, Toronto, Ontario, Canada M6K 3H6

Distributed in the U.K. by Guild of Master Craftsman Publications Ltd.,
Castle Place, 166 High Street, Lewes, East Sussex, England BN7 1XU
Tel: (+ 44) 1273 477374, Fax: (+ 44) 1273 478606,
Email: pubs@thegmcgroup.com, Web: www.gmcpublications.com

Distributed in Australia by Capricorn Link (Australia) Pty Ltd.,
P.O. Box 704, Windsor, NSW 2756 Australia

If you have questions or comments about this book, please contact:
Lark Books, 67 Broadway, Asheville, NC 28801, (828) 253-0467

Manufactured in China

ISBN 1-57990-536-6

contents

Is knitting the perfect craft?

As a stress-reducing creative endeavor, wonderfully compact and portable, knitting has no peer. In this fast-paced, competitive world, knitting is a great respite from the pressure and transitory nature of modern life. But even more precious is the magic transformation that happens when, with two sticks and some string, you create a beautiful knitted accessory that transcends its humble origins. Women and men—professionals and students, moms and dads, young 20-somethings, have discovered (or rediscovered) knitting. An amazing variety of yarns has created even more interest in knitting, as yarn lovers ask themselves, what can I do with this fabulous yarn—quickly and easily?

As avid and serious knitters ourselves, we wrote *Exquisite Little Knits* in order to present 40 fabulous and quick-to-knit scarves, hats, purses, and more in the most luxurious, surprising, and delightful yarns you've ever laid hands and eyes on. These are projects that can travel anywhere you do. Knitting on the go is a great way to maximize your time and reduce the tedium of waiting. We've knit on bumpy bus rides, at the subway station, in doctors' offices. We've purled at soccer games, on long car trips, and waiting for babies to be born. Not only have we made the most of our precious time, we've made instant friends—and potential new knitters—as they asked questions about the unusual yarns we favor. But these benefits pale in comparison to the pride we feel when we're wearing luxurious and fashionable accessories we've crafted ourselves.

And though some designs are flirtatiously modish, there's nothing outlandish here. These are simply beautiful expressions of the craft, using innovative yet easy techniques to let the yarns get all the attention. In fact, we have a saying: Let the yarn do the work. It means that the yarn creates the pattern. Very little fancy stitch work is required (stitch work takes time and concentration, precious but limited commodities). Instead, the yarn elevates simple stitches to a whole new level.

We believe that the yarn you use is probably the most significant decision you're likely to make about how the finished product inherently looks and feels, so we organized the book by fiber type. Some are tried-and-true standards and others are upstart newcomers. The nine fiber chapters explore the wonders of wool, cashmere and qiviut, ribbon, mohair and angora, silk, eyelash and fur, lattice, sequin, and suede. Throughout the book you'll find suggestions and notes for how to best use these yarns in your

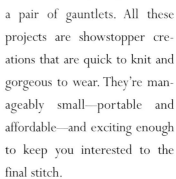

knitting. We've included a few tips about the qualities of the materials and made suggestions for the most appropriate needles.

Many designs here will enhance your wardrobe: narrow ties that wrap your neck or drape down to your knees, wide stoles for bare shoulders. Other pieces will ignite your imagination, such as special little purses, hats, and even a pair of gauntlets. All these projects are showstopper creations that are quick to knit and gorgeous to wear. They're manageably small—portable and affordable—and exciting enough to keep you interested to the final stitch.

Whether you've been knitting since childhood, are thinking about a return to a long-lost skill, or you've never knitted before, you're guaranteed to have a great time making these accessories. We know we did.

LAURIE KIMMELSTIEL AND IRIS SCHREIER

basics

Walk into any yarn shop these days and you'll be mesmerized by all the beautiful and unique fibers on display. To keep pace with the booming popularity of hand knitting, yarns are becoming more spectacular every season. But this question always arises: What can you make with these yarns? We've faced the same challenge ourselves, and we want to share some of our solutions for achieving knitting nirvana. In this chapter, we'll point out techniques to create one-of-a-kind knitted accessories worthy of the most luxurious fibers.

Enter our knitting heaven and explore the world of glorious fiber. We have found some of the most exotic yarns for the designs in our book. With origins from Peru to the Far East, these yarns are more accessible than ever, whether at your local yarn purveyor or through one of the many online fiber boutiques.

◆ ◆ ◆ ◆

It never hurts to review the basic qualities of yarns, no matter how fancy or plain. Characteristics such as fiber weight, elasticity and drape, luster, hand and texture, color, and fiber type all play a role in determining what sort of pattern works best with which yarn.

Weight refers to the thickness as well as the weighed heft of the yarn. It's usually determined by calculating the yardage (or the weighed amount) per skein, ball, or hank. For example, a thin or fine yarn generally includes more yards in a standard ball than does a thick or heavy yarn. You'll want to use a fine yarn in projects that call for more detailed work, because it will show off the design better. For the quickest, easiest projects, knit heavy weight yarn with larger needles. Some of the fibers used in this book, such as lattice, ribbon, and sequin yarns, aren't categorized by their weight at all. The term can seem a bit vague, so your best indicator of a yarn's weight is in the relationship of the weighed amount to its yardage.

The stretchiness of the fiber is called *elasticity*. Pull on the strand to see if it becomes longer and, more important, whether it bounces back. Incredibly, totally inelastic yarns, such as ribbon and cotton, often knit up into fabrics that are very elastic, so stretchiness can't be determined solely by examining the unknitted fiber; the weave of the knitted piece will impart a certain degree of elasticity. If a knitted yarn has *give*, another term for elasticity, it's usually more "forgiving" and therefore easier for a beginner knitter, who might have a tendency

SKILL LEVELS

◆ · · ·
Beginner

◆ ◆ · ·
Easy

◆ ◆ ◆ ·
Intermediate

◆ ◆ ◆ ◆
Experienced

to tense up when first learning to knit. The fibers that lack elasticity are better suited to those more experienced in the craft.

Luster is the brightness of yarn as it shines with reflected light. Yarn luster comes in all varieties ranging from bright to dull. Some fibers are so lustrous they have a kind of "wet" look, while others are matte, with a smooth finish that has limited shine, or none at all. Use matte yarn for a dressed-down, subtle effect, and glossy yarn for a dressy look. The Trellis Stole on page 64 was knitted both ways so you can see what a difference luster makes. Another option is to add interest to a project by mixing yarns with different lustrous qualities. For example, the Honey Bear Hat on page 123 contrasts shiny rayon with matte merino wool.

Try knitting a large swatch in your pattern stitch and check the fabric to determine the *drape* of your fiber. How does it fall? Is it stiff or limp?

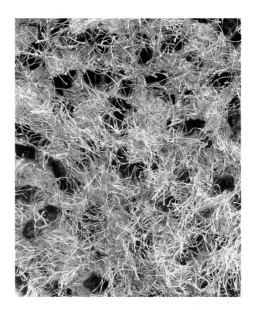

Does it bunch up or hang down neatly on its own? Perhaps you need to knit the piece on larger or smaller needles. Changing the needle size—or even the needle type—can make all the difference between a piece that lies properly and one that hangs stiffly or awkwardly. Maybe you can add another yarn to improve how the fabric falls. For example, the ribbon edging on the Romantic Ruffled Scarf (page 70) is a decorative element, but it also provides more body and structure to the somewhat fluttery ends of the knitted mohair. The result is an improved overall drape of the finished garment.

Check the *hand*—those appealing tactile qualities of texture, fineness, and durability—of the fiber. Some stiffer or coarser fibers are better suited for accessories, such as purses or vests, that won't come in direct contact with your skin. Other, softer fibers, such as cashmere and qiviut,

are perfect right next to the body, as seen in our Soft and Snug Gauntlets on page 34.

Texture can vary dramatically from smooth to loopy and everything in between—even within similar fiber categories. Is it coarse or soft to the touch? Flat yarns, such as ribbons, and others, like the carrier-thread yarns with extra fibers that jut out from them, can enhance whatever yarn they're combined with. In general, the more texture in the fiber, the larger the needles you'll need to guarantee that the yarn's unique characteristics aren't crushed or buried in the fabric.

Color variations depend on the methods used to dye the yarn as well as on the fiber itself. The same color can appear muted in one type of yarn and vivid in another. Variations in color between dye lots are not uncommon, so be sure to pur-

chase a sufficient quantity in one dye lot before you begin a project. It's likely that you won't be able to buy more later, because many yarns go in and out of fashion as quickly as bellbottom pants.

Fiber type refers to the source of the yarn—specifically, whether the yarn is of protein, plant, or synthetic origin. Wool, silk, rayon, and other animal fibers and plant fibers, including cotton and linen, are all considered natural fibers. Synthetics include nylon (polyamide), acrylic, and polyester.

Wool varies in texture depending largely on the breed of the sheep, and we love merino wool, primarily because of its softness. Merino also has a beautiful luster and a good amount of elasticity, and, not surprisingly, it's a wonderful yarn for a beginner knitter.

By far the warmest, lightest, and most luxurious yarns for hand knitters are cashmere and qiviut (KIV-ee-uht). While cashmere comes from the soft, fine under-coat of the goat, qiviut is taken from the undercoat of the musk ox. Due to its incredibly soft hand, this type of yarn often looks best knitted in a tex-tured pattern or in stitch types that are found in rib, seed stitch, or basket weave patterns that use both knit and purl stitches in the same row.

Mohair also comes from goats, while angora is plucked from rabbits. Both fibers are naturally fuzzy and provide incredible warmth despite their light weight. Mohair can almost always be knitted on needles larger than you would expect to use with yarns of similar size and weight. Both mohair and angora have a unique *loft* that spreads the fiber as it's knitted and can produce very dense garments.

Silk, a filament extruded by silkworms of certain moths, is a lustrous fiber with good drape and little elasticity. While believed to be warmer than wool, silk can also produce sheer, cool fab-rics suitable for all climates. Silk lends strength and character to yarn when it's spun together with other fibers. Many of the yarns used in this book are silk blends.

Rayon, a manufactured natural fiber that is often very shiny, is strong and has a beautiful drape. It's a component of several of the specialty yarns we've used here, including faux suede, sequin, and some of the ribbon types.

Many man-made fibers offer interesting tex-tures and colors not readily found in natural fibers, including slub, chainette, eyelash, railroad, loop, tube, polka dot, plaited rib-bon, metallic, and filigree yarns. We care-fully chose these exotic yarns for many of the designs created for this book. Synthetics aren't necessarily of lesser quality—even among artificial fibers you'll find a range of grades, so choose them with care. Experiment. Some of these unusual yarns produce unexpected results, such as the Bumblebee Shawl on page 62. Some will create softer fabrics, others might offer a lighter drape, and, of course, these fibers offer the most unique and unusual opportunities for creative knitting.

Although the designs included in this book, if followed exactly, will ensure exciting and dramatic results, we urge you to consider them as starting points. Think about using other yarns and making modifications to the patterns as needed. Here are some tips to ensure a successful outcome.

If the design doesn't look right with the substitute yarn you've chosen, experiment by making small swatches with different stitch combinations. Put together unexpected color combinations—combine two different textured yarns in related colors, such as in the Gemstone Scarf on page 66. You'll be amazed at how different the knitted result looks from the two yarns that went into it. We knitted some of our projects in an alternate version so you could see just how versatile and rewarding using different yarns can be. We've also shown close-up photos of the individual strands of yarn used in every project to guide you in creating your own versions.

The incredible variations and selections of yarns now available are yours to enjoy and play with. But beware ... as you knit these beautiful accessories, expect to get requests from friends and relatives for knitted gifts. Strangers may even offer to buy them from you! Most important, knit something you love and cherish it for years to come. And always be on the lookout for rare, unusual, and exotic luxury fibers to create accessories that will enhance any wardrobe.

A Few Words about Needles   Knitting needles can be found in varied sizes and an interesting selection of configurations or types. They are available in an array of materials, including aluminum, brass, nickel, wood, bamboo, and casein.

Needles range in diameter from 0.75mm to 25mm and are generally marked with their metric measurement. Those manufactured in the United States also have U.S. sizes on them, and the U.K. has its own sizing system (see the needle chart, at left). If you find it difficult to read the size on the needle, or if the printed size has rubbed off, a needle gauge will come in handy.

Certain needle types are more suitable for particular projects and yarns. We've suggested needles for some designs in which the type or composition of the tool can make a difference in your comfort and ease while knitting. For instance, needles made from dark exotic wood can help you knit a fine, light yarn; the contrast between the two eases the task. We find that slippery yarns often work best on wood or bamboo, whereas coarser fibers move more effortlessly and seem to knit up more quickly on the shiny nickel-coated aluminum or brass.

Circular needles are our personal preference and are suitable for most projects. These ingenious needles are comprised of two short needles joined by a nylon cord. With these you can knit flat, just as you would with ordinary straight needles, or you can knit "in the round" for seamless garments, such as in our North Cape Balaclava on page 56. Circulars also offer a host of other advantages, including compactness that allows you to knit on the go and a design that keeps your stitches from slipping off your needles. Some say that they put less stress on the wrists too.

Experiment by knitting with various types of needles and different fibers. You may find that you prefer wood or bamboo needles to better control your knitting, or that you like to speed it up with nickel or aluminum. Use the needle type that you find most comfortable. If we recommend bamboo and you prefer nickel or plastic, go ahead. We can only recommend the products that have worked best for us. And, similarly, if you prefer straight and we've suggested circular, use the straight ones, unless the design requires a specific needle type, such as with some of our hats and purses. Remember, if you use straight needles for a circular project, you'll need to sew together the edges into a seam.

Needle length applies to straight, circular, and double-pointed needles alike. Choose the shortest possible needles that are practical for your particular project. You may find that the cords on longer circular needles may become curled and twisted when knitting some of the smaller projects. With the exception of our large shawls or scarves knit lengthwise, most of our designs can be completed using shorter needles. Personally, we love 16-inch (40.6cm) circulars because they're convenient to use and you can tuck them away very nicely in your purse or knitting bag. You'll also find that despite their short length you can still get quite a few stitches on them.

Another point—or, rather, points—is that some circular needles have longer or sharper ends than others. These can be a hazard to you and your knitwear, so consider your yarn type when choosing the needles for your project. With ribbon yarns in particular, but also with those fibers lacking a tight twist, sharp tips can poke small holes in the fiber. These longer, sharper ends may also be a source of additional stress to the hands and wrists. To prevent stitches from inadvertently slipping off the needles, use point protectors to store your unfinished projects. For easy reference, sort and store your circular needles by size or length in labeled, see-through bags.

Check out how your circular needle is attached to the cord. Many times the seam line or join can be a sticking point—literally. Your stitches may catch here, and you'll be constantly tugging at your work. This may limit your ability to maintain rhythmic knitting or, worse, prompt you to give up in frustration. Therefore, choose your needles carefully and replace those that don't provide smooth sailing for your stitches.

Great needles are those that you prefer even if you have a half-dozen others in the same size. The industry is always inventing new technical advances and exciting new materials for faster, easier knitting. Check out some of these products and materials and you may discover something that's just right for your creative knitting hands. Even experienced knitters like us continuously experiment with different needle products in search of that perfect device for our favorite craft. Invest in these just as you do with your yarns; after all, luxury fibers deserve top-notch tools.

Knitter's Necessities   Every knitter deserves a roomy, stylish knitting bag. In addition, you'll also require some smaller containers or pouches to separate your various projects and knitting supplies.

Heavy-duty zipper-type plastic bags make ideal enclosures for small tools and works in progress. Keep another sturdy see-through bag for the myriad other accessories that are so necessary for knitters on the go. These include a tape measure (we recommend a spring-type cloth or metal version that retracts into a small box), small scissors that fold into themselves or have a plastic or leather protector over the points, and a crochet hook for weaving in ends. A supply of stitch holders, stitch markers, a tapestry needle, pins for fastening seams, and some nongreasy hand cream round out your basic knitter's tool kit.

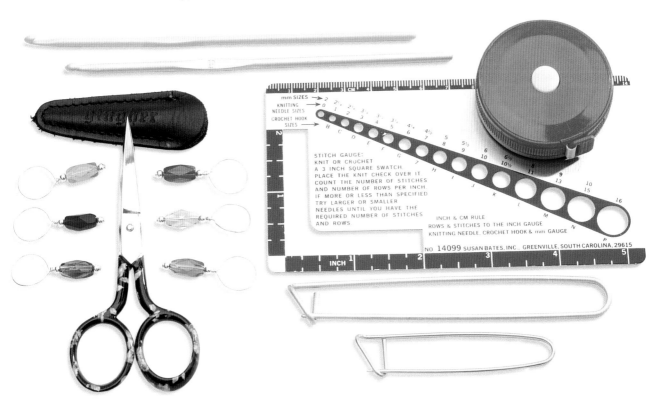

Techniques A few special techniques are used in this book. A novice knitter may want to try some of our more advanced projects, and we encourage it. The standard knitting techniques referred to here that may be unfamiliar to a beginner can be found in any good how-to-knit book.

Transferring to Double-Pointed Needles from Circular Needles

Count your stitches and divide that number more or less equally by three or four, according to the number of double-pointed needles (dpn) called for in the pattern. (Double-pointed needles are sold in sets of either four or five, depending on the manufacturer.) Knit that number of stitches from your circular needle onto the first double-pointed one. Knit the next group of stitches onto another double-pointed needle, and so on, until you've completely transferred the row.

Placing Markers on Double-Pointed Needles

Any markers placed at the end of double-pointed needles are sure to fall off. You have two choices: you can put point protectors on the tips of each end of the needles or move your stitches on the needles so that at least one stitch is on either side of a marker. To avoid confusion and to help remember which marker indicates the end of a row, consider using a larger or smaller marker here, or another color to help you differentiate.

Double-Knit Pattern

Double knitting as it's used in this book creates a reversible fabric with knit stitches facing out on both sides of the work. You'll knit on both sides at the same time, and the result is a two-layer fabric. You will always use two different-color yarns for the double-knitted projects in this book.

Colors A and B are always used together to cast on. Whenever AB is specified in the instructions, knit or purl with both strands together. Whenever A or B are specified separately, knit or purl with the individual strands.

Our double-knit patterns have been designed in such a way that after the first row you won't need to refer to any charts or patterns. After

photo 1

photo 2

you've turned the work to start the next row, just knit the knit stitches and purl the purl stitches, using the same color strand that was used in the previous row as it now faces you. The most important thing to remember is that when knitting you should bring both strands to the back, and when purling bring both strands to the front.

Here's how to do this: Keep color B strand above color A strand so that you can more easily knit with color A and purl with color B. Hold both strands behind the work when knitting (photo 1) and hold them both in front of the work when purling, as shown in photo 2. Try to keep the strands from twisting while you maneuver them from front to back, knitting A and purling B separately.

If you've never used this technique before, practice with two identical yarns in two contrast-ing colors to create a swatch. Comments follow the sample instructions given here:

CO 12 sts with AB

Hold two strands together, one of each color (A and B)

Row 1: K1 AB, (k1 A, p1 B) 5 times, k1 AB

    Knit 1 with both AB in the first stitch. Alternate knitting 1 with A, and purling 1 with B, for a total of 5 times. Knit 1 with both AB in the last stitch, for a total of 12 sts.

Row 2: K1 AB, (k1 B, p1 A) 5 times, k1 AB

    This row is the same as row 1, except now you'll knit with B and purl with A.

Repeat rows 1 and 2, and you'll see how you've created two separate layers of fabric at the same time. If the stitches appear uneven, use smaller needles than the ones specified in the pattern.

photo 3

photo 4

photo 5

photo 6

MAKING FRINGE

Using the number and length of strands specified in the project, hold the strands together evenly, folding them in half to make a loop. Insert a large crochet hook into the garment where you'll be applying the fringe and catch all the strands in the center.

Draw the loop end through (photo 3), making it large enough so you can pull the ends of the yarn through the loop (photo 4). Pull down on the ends so the loops tighten snugly around the stitch.

MAKING TASSELS

Follow project directions regarding the exact length and number of strands; one strand should be longer than the others. Insert a large crochet hook into the stitch in which the tassel is to be inserted. Draw one end of the cut strands through

figure 1

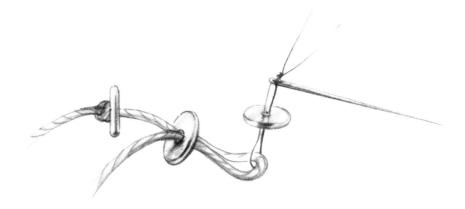

this stitch, making sure that they hang evenly on both sides of the stitch, with the exception of one end of the longer strands, as shown in photo 5. Wrap the longer strand around the others 5 times (photo 6).

Insert a small crochet hook up into the tassel, catch the piece of longer strand that has been wrapping around the tassel, and pull it through so that it hangs down with the remaining strands. Trim if necessary to even all the lengths.

Attaching Beads or Sequins to Tassels

Thread a small piece—about 3"/8cm—of sewing thread of any color onto a sewing needle. Tie the thread ends to make a loop.

Choose one strand from the tassel, passing about 1"/1.6mm of the strand through the sewing-thread loop. String a sequin or bead onto the sewing needle, over the sewing-thread loop and onto the tassel's yarn strand. Tie a knot in the yarn strand so that a sequin or bead can rest just above it (figure 1). Add more sequins or beads in this way, staggering their placement as needed for an interesting effect.

Ribbon Wrapping

Weave the ribbon instead of knitting with it, bringing it forward and in front of all knit stitches and sending it behind all purl stitches (photos 7 and 8 on page 22). Make sure to stretch out the knitted work at the completion of each row to keep the ribbon from tightening the fabric.

photo 7

photo 8

photo 9

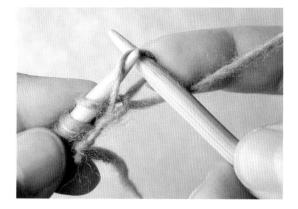

photo 10

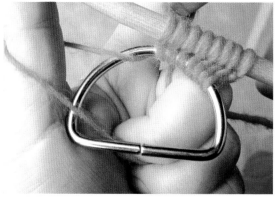

KNITTED CAST ON

Make a slip knot. Insert the tip of your right-hand needle into the stitch and knit into it, leaving the original stitch on the left-hand needle. Pass the loop you just made on the right-hand needle onto the left-hand one, as shown in photo 9.

Repeat by inserting the tip of the right-hand needle into the newly formed loop, or stitch, on the left-hand needle. Knit into that stitch, leaving the original stitch on the left-hand needle. Pass the new loop you just made on the right-hand needle back onto the left-hand needle. Repeat this process for the specified number of stitches.

CASTING ON TO A BELT RING

Thread the yarn over your fingers and through the belt ring, as shown in photo 10, leaving enough of a tail for the number of stitches you'll be casting on. Cast on one stitch (photo 11 on page 23) then snug the yarn against the needle and the belt ring

photo 11

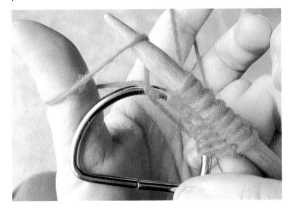

photo 12

photo 13

photo 14

(photo 12). Before casting on the next stitch, pull the short tail through to the front of the ring.

BINDING OFF FROM A BELT RING

Cut the yarn, leaving a tail long enough to complete the binding off (for 8 stitches, leave a minimum of 10–20"/25–50cm). Hold the ring behind the knitting while binding off. Attach it to the first stitch as follows: Pass the tail yarn through the ring (away from you) and into the position to knit. Insert the right-hand needle into the stitch on the left-hand needle and, using the tail yarn, knit 1.

*Pass the tail yarn back through the ring, away from you. Insert the right-hand needle into the next stitch on the left-hand needle and use the tail yarn to knit 1. Bind off as usual. Repeat the process from * until you bind off all stitches. Pass the tail through the last loop on your needle and pull the tail to tighten, as in photo 14.

CASHMERE
& qiviut

Of all of the wonderful yarns we've worked with for this book, cashmere and qiviut are probably the most luxe. For generations cashmere has been the yarn of style and status, but its ultrasoft texture can be a challenge to knit with and it deserves exceptional stitch arrangements. The textured stitches and double-knitting techniques used in this chapter show off cashmere's most alluring characteristics and provide a new approach to this traditional fiber.

Qiviut is an extraordinary yarn, even more rare than cashmere, that's simply yummy—a joy to handle and knit. This delicate fiber provides lots of warmth without the weight or scratchiness of other fibers. Qiviut is less elastic than wool and not nearly as fuzzy as its counterparts, cashmere and alpaca. Quite frankly, we haven't found anything quite as luxurious as this fiber.

. . . .

Dewdrops Scarf

DESIGN BY
IRIS SCHREIER

SKILL LEVEL
◆ ◆ ◆ ◆
Beginner

This simple but beautiful design is ideal for any multicolored cashmere. Like dewdrops on a windowpane, knit and purl stitches are evenly dispersed to provide thickness and texture that enhance the scarf's drape, and the pattern stitch best shows off the hand-painted palette of the striking yarn.

FINISHED MEASUREMENTS
80 x 6"/203 x 15cm

MATERIALS
Approx total: 300yd/274m light weight cashmere or cashmere blend yarn in variegated, multicolor
Knitting needles: 5.5mm (size 9 U.S.) *or size to obtain gauge*

GAUGE
22 sts and 29 rows = 4"/10cm in Seed Stitch
Always take time to check your gauge.

INSTRUCTIONS
CO 33 sts.

BORDER PATTERN
Rows 1–3: K.
Rows 4–8: K1, p1 across.
Rows 9–11: K.

SCARF BODY
Row 12: K1, p1 across.
Rep row 12 until scarf is 78½"/199cm or desired length.
End by repeating rows 1–11 of Border Pattern.
BO all sts. Cut yarn and weave in ends.

THIS PROJECT WAS KNIT WITH
1 skein of Knit 'n Tyme's *Makalu Cashmere 4-ply DK Handpainted*, 100% cashmere, DK weight, 3.5oz/100g = approx 350yd/320m, color Enchanted

Winter
Squares
Scarf

DESIGN BY
IRIS SCHREIER

SKILL LEVEL
◆ ◆ ◇ ◇
Easy

Don't let this scarf's deep, rugged texture fool you; it's as soft and light as can be. The two yarns are subtly twisted together in the center, with both colors carried through from row to row. You won't need to cut the yarn until you've completed the scarf, saving you the work of weaving in a lot of ends. Best of all, the scarf is completely reversible.

FINISHED MEASUREMENTS
86 x 5"/218 x 13cm

MATERIALS
Approx total: 260yd/238m cashmere or cashmere blend chunky weight yarn
Color A: 130yd/119m in gray tweed
Color B: 130yd/119m in natural
Knitting needles: 8mm (size 11 U.S.) *or size to obtain gauge*

GAUGE
11 sts and 13 rows = 4"/10cm in Garter Stitch
Always take time to check your gauge.

INSTRUCTIONS
Note: The gray tweed squares are worked in Garter Stitch; the natural squares are worked in Seed Stitch. The two yarns are always twisted in the center of the scarf, in the same direction and on the same side. To avoid holes when switching colors, make sure to twist the yarns as specified in the instructions. For example, if A is in the front, twist it over and around B, bringing A from the front to the back. If A is in the back, twist it over and around B, bringing A from the back to the front.

With A, CO 14 sts.

FIRST PAIR OF SQUARES
Row 1: With A, k7. Do not cut A; attach B, and with B, *k1, p1; work from * total of 3 times, k1.
Row 2: With B, *k1, p1; work from * total of 3 times, k1. With B in front, twist B over and around A. With A, k7.
Row 3: With A, k7. With A in back, twist A over and around B. With B, *k1, p1; work from * total of 3 times, k1.
Rows 4–9: Rep rows 2–3 three times.

Row 10: Repeat row 2.
Row 11: With A, k7. With A in back, twist A over and around B. With A, k7.

SECOND PAIR OF SQUARES
Row 12: With A, k7. With A in front, twist A over and around B. With B, *k1, p1; work from * total of 3 times, k1.
Row 13: With B, *k1, p1; work from * total of 3 times, k1. With B in back, twist B over and around A. With A, k7.
Rows 14–19: Rep rows 12–13 three times.
Row 20: With A, k7. With A in front, twist A over and around B. With A, k7.

Rep 1st and 2nd pairs of squares (rows 2–20) until the scarf measures 86"/2.2m or desired length. With A, BO all sts. Cut yarn and weave ends.

THIS PROJECT WAS KNIT WITH
A 2 skeins of Classic Elite's *Forbidden*, 100% cashmere, chunky weight, 1.8oz/50g = approx 65yd/59m per skein, color #60550 Marled Storm

B 2 skeins of Classic Elite's *Forbidden,* 100% cashmere, chunky weight, 1.8oz/50g = approx 65yd/59m per skein, color #10015 White

B

A

Jewel-Tone Wrap

DESIGN BY
IRIS SCHREIER

SKILL LEVEL
◆ ◆ ◇ ◇
Easy

Pashmina shawls are so popular that we felt compelled to include our own version of the ultimate cashmere wrap. To enhance this particular variegated yarn, we developed an open mesh design that gives the shawl body and shape. Because the staggered, openwork stitch orients the knitted fabric in one direction and then is reversed midway to slant the other way, special shaping isn't needed. The shawl naturally knits up into a perfect V shape.

FINISHED MEASUREMENTS
70 x 20"/178 x 51cm

MATERIALS
Approx total: 600yd/549m cashmere or cashmere blend superfine weight yarn in variegated, plum
Knitting needles: 5.5mm (size 9 U.S.) *or size to obtain gauge*

GAUGE
13½ sts and 27 rows = 4"/10cm
Always take time to check your gauge.

INSTRUCTIONS
CO 67 sts.
Rows 1–3: K1, p1, k1, k to last 3 sts, k1, p1, k1.
Row 4: K1, p1, k2, *yo, skkp; rep from * to last 3 sts, k1, p1, k1.
Row 5: K1, p1, k1, p to last 3 sts, k1, p1, k1.
Row 6: K1, p1, k3, *yo, skkp; rep from * to last 5 sts, k3, p1, k1.
Row 7: K1, p1, k1, p to last 3 sts, k1, p1, k1.
Row 8: K1, p1, k1, *yo, skkp; rep from * to last 4 sts, k2, p1, k1.
Row 9: K1, p1, k1, p to last 3 sts, k1, p1, k1.

Rep rows 4–9, ending with row 8 when the shawl measures 35"/89cm, or one-half of desired total length of shawl.
Then reverse direction as follows:
Row 1: K1, p1, k1, p1, *yo, sppp; rep from * to last 3 sts, k1, p1, k1.

Row 2: K1, p1, k1, k to last 3 sts, k1, p1, k1.
Row 3: K1, p1, k1, p2, *yo, sppp; rep from * to last 5 sts, p2, k1, p1, k1.
Row 4: K1, p1, k1, k to last 3 sts, k1, p1, k1.
Row 5: K1, p1, k1, *yo, sppp; rep from * to last 4 sts, p1, k1, p1, k1.
Row 6: K1, p1, k1, k to last 3 sts, k1, p1, k1.

Rep rows 1–6, ending with row 5 when shawl measures nearly 70"/178cm, and rep row 6 three more times for bottom trim. BO, cut yarn, and weave in ends.

THIS PROJECT WAS KNIT WITH
7 hanks of Mountain Colors' Cashmere, 100% cashmere, fingering weight, 1oz/28g = approx 95yd/87m per hank, color Wild Raspberry

Russian Tiger Cap

DESIGN BY
LAURIE KIMMELSTIEL

SKILL LEVEL
◆ ◆ ◇ ◇

Easy

The deep brim on this thick and stretchy cashmere cap is perfect for a frigid winter day. (It reminds me of those bulky Russian fur hats worn in *Dr. Zhivago*.) I chose a color scheme that mimics a tiger's coloration. You'll find that the simple Garter Stitch design makes the hat very easy and quick to knit.

FINISHED MEASUREMENTS
19 x 16"/48 x 20cm
(before seams are sewn)

MATERIALS
Approx total: 440yd/402m cashmere or cashmere blend medium weight yarn
Color A: 220yd/201m in brown
Color B: 220yd/201m in black
Knitting needles: 6.5mm (size 10½ U.S.), nickel-plated needles recommended, *or size to obtain gauge*
Tapestry needle for sewing seams
Pins for fastening seams

GAUGE
9¼ sts and 12 rows = 4"/10cm in Garter Stitch
Always take time to check your gauge.

INSTRUCTIONS
Note: A and B are worked together throughout. The hat is knitted flat, then the edges sewn to form the finished shape.

With A and B tog, CO 44 sts.

HAT BODY
Row 1: K.
Rep row 1 until piece measures 10¼"/31cm.

HAT TOP
Row 1: *K2tog, k7, k2tog; rep from * to end—36 sts.
Row 2: K.
Row 3: *K2tog, k5, k2tog; rep from * to end—28 sts.
Row 4: K.
Row 5: *K2tog, k3, k2tog; rep from * to end—20 sts.

Row 6: K.
Row 7: *K2tog, k1, k2tog; rep from * to end—12 sts.
Row 8: K.
Row 9: *K2tog; rep from * to end—6 sts.

Cut yarn, leaving 18"/46cm tail. Thread yarn in tapestry needle; slip tapestry needle through rem 6 sts in row 9 and pull thread through.

Pin edges and sew tog, being careful to fold brim over. Stitch brim (4"/10cm rollover edge) on reverse side. Cut yarn and weave in ends.

THIS PROJECT WAS KNIT WITH
A 1 skein of Joseph Galler's *Mimosa*, 85% cashmere/15% nylon, worsted weight, 3.6oz/100g = approx 220yd/201m, color Beaver

B 1 skein of Joseph Galler's *Mimosa*, 85% cashmere/15% nylon, worsted weight, 3.6oz/100g = approx 220yd/201m, color Black

A

B

Soft and Snug Gauntlets

DESIGN BY
LAURIE KIMMELSTIEL

SKILL LEVEL

◆ ◆ ◇ ◇

Easy

These lightweight gaunt-
lets, sort of sweater
sleeves ending in half-
gloves, are newly popular
accessories. Wear them
in cool weather with a
sleeveless top or on a
chillier day when you
need to keep your fingers
free to drive—or even
knit! The narrow ribbed
bands on the forearm and
at mid-hand keep them
firmly in place. This design
narrows a bit at the wrist
for a custom fit.

Finished Measurements
12½ x 8½"/32 x 22cm (before seams are sewn)

Materials
Approx total: 400yd/366m qiviut or qiviut blend, superfine weight yarn
Color A: 200yd/183m in variegated red
Color B: 200yd/183m in brown
Knitting needles: 3.75mm (size 5 U.S.); also 4.25mm (size 6 U.S.) *or size to obtain gauge*; wood or bamboo recommended
Pins for fastening seams
Tapestry needle for sewing seams

Gauge
19¾ sts and 40 rows = 4"/10cm in Pattern Stitch
Always take time to check your gauge.

Instructions
Note: Yarns A and B are alternated; the yarn not in use remains attached at the end of the row.
With larger needles and A, CO 42 sts. Change to smaller needles. Start with Rib Stitch.

Rib Stitch
Row 1: With smaller needles and A, k2, p2 across.
Row 2: P2, k2 across.
Row 3: Rep row 1.
Change to B as foll: don't tie a knot, but p the 1st 3 sts, using both A and B to secure B. Cont to p across the row, using B only.
Next row: With B, p.

Pattern Stitch
Row 1(RS): With A, k.
Row 2: Rep row 1.
Row 3: With B, p.
Row 4: Rep row 3.

Gauntlet Body
Rep rows 1–4 of Pattern Stitch until piece measures approx 5¼"/13cm, ending with row 4.
Dec over 6 rows as foll:
Row 1: With A, k1, skp, k to last 3 sts, k2tog, k1—40 sts.
Row 2: With A, k.
Row 3: With B, p1, spp, p to last 3 sts of row, p2tog, p1—38 sts.
Row 4: With B, p.
Row 5: With A, k1, skp, k to last 3 sts, k2tog, k1—36 sts.
Row 6: With A, k.

Cont in rows 1–4 of Pattern Stitch until piece measures 10"/25cm or desired length to wrist.

Hand Increase
Row 1(RS): With A, k1, k1inc1, k to end—37 sts.
Row 2: Rep row 1—38 sts.
Row 3: With B, p1, p1inc1, p to end—39 sts.
Row 4: Rep row 3—40 sts.
Rep rows 1–4 until 50 sts.

Cont in rows 1–4 of Pattern Stitch until piece measures 12¼"/31cm or desired length, ending with row 4 of Pattern Stitch. With A, work 3 rows of Rib Stitch as above, then use the 4.25mm needle to BO very loosely. Cut yarn.

Lightly press the edges of the finished piece with a cool iron and pin the gauntlet tog lengthwise with WS out and horizontal stripes aligned. Thread the tapestry needle and sew the gauntlet edges tog, joining them neatly and smoothly. Turn the gauntlet to RS and, with the seam facing the middle of the palm of your right hand, try it on. Remove gauntlet. To create an opening for the thumb, sew several small sts at the top edge between the thumb and forefinger, 1½"/4cm in from the thumb. Cut yarn. Weave in ends. Repeat for left hand.

This project was knit with
A   1 skein of Artyarns' *Modular Qiviut*, 100% qiviut, fingering weight, 0.9oz/25g = approx 210yd/192m, color Sedona Red
B   1 ball of Jacques Cartier Clothier's *Qiviuk*, 100% qiviut, fingering weight, 1.8oz/50g = approx 420yd/384m, color Natural Brown

A

B

Racing
Stripes
Scarf

DESIGN BY
IRIS SCHREIER

SKILL LEVEL
◆ ◆ ◆ ◆
Intermediate

Only when you hold the knitted piece in your hands will you know the unbelievable softness of this double-faced scarf. It's ideal for fingering or fine weight cashmere because the two layers create a very soft drape. Choose your own combination of contrasting colors for a strong fashion statement.

FINISHED MEASUREMENTS
66 x 5"/168 x 13cm

MATERIALS
Approx total: 300yd/274m cashmere or cashmere blend superfine weight yarn
Color A: 150yd/137m in blue
Color B: 150yd/137m in black
Knitting needles: 4.5mm (size 7 U.S.) *or size to obtain gauge*

GAUGE
32 sts and 25 rows = 4"/10cm in Double-Knit Pattern
Always take time to check your gauge.

INSTRUCTIONS

Note: The pattern is worked throughout using 1 strand A and 1 strand B. A and B strands are knitted together when instructions specify AB, and knitted and purled separately when instructions specify only A or B. When knitting A or B separately take both colors to the back, and when purling A or B separately take both colors to the front. If this is your first time using this technique, refer to the Double-Knit Pattern technique on page 18.

CO 40 sts with AB.

Row 1: K1 AB, *(k1 A, p1 B) 3 times, (k1 B, p1 A) once; rep from * to last 1 st, K1 AB—40 sts
Row 2: K1 AB, *(k1 B, p1 A) 3 times, (k1 A, p1 B) once; rep from * to last st, K1 AB—40 sts
Rep rows 1 and 2 until scarf measures 66"/168cm or desired length.

BO using AB, k the knit sts and p the purl sts.
Cut yarn and weave in ends.

THIS PROJECT WAS KNIT WITH
A 1 hank of Joseph Galler's *Pashmina*, 100% cashmere, 1.8oz/50gm = approx 170yd/155m, color Glacier Blue
B 1 hank of Joseph Galler's *Pashmina*, 100% cashmere, 1.8oz/50gm = approx 170yd/155m, color Black

A

B

ALTERNATE
This photo shows the project knit with Schoeller's *Stahl Fortissima*, 100% wool, colors Socka #9095 and #9073

EYELASH
fur

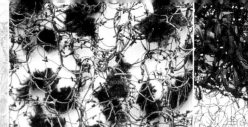

These yarns opened us up to a world of creativity, offering possibilities previously unimaginable in the average knitter's realm. Because these yarns mimic objects found in nature, we were able to design garments that seem to defy explanation. They frequently spark comments such as "You didn't knit that, did you?" and "What is that made of?"

We had loads of fun creating these extraordinary designs. At heart they're simple scarves and shawls that make any outfit remarkable. The yarns require little in the way of complicated patterning or difficult stitches. Many of these fibers are available in an array of unusual colors, and we implore you to try them all! With a little practice (yes, they take some getting used to), you'll fall in love with them too.

To familiarize yourself with the fibers, we recommend that you knit a swatch first. Eyelash and fur yarns tend to be stretchy. Keep this in mind, especially for those designs that call for two yarns knitted together. You may want to experiment until you feel at ease with their give. Wood or bamboo needles are best—especially for filigree yarns—because the narrow fibers tend to slip too easily off other types of needles. Moisturize your hands with a nongreasy hand cream so that dry skin won't catch on these fancy fibers.

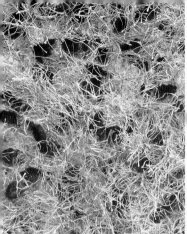

Polka Dot Scarfette

DESIGN BY
LAURIE KIMMELSTIEL

SKILL LEVEL
◆ ◆ ◇ ◇

Easy

Do you have an extra hour on your hands? This three-pointed little "scarfette" is a very quick and easy project. Iris and I loved knitting it in lots of different colors. We combine it with a funky Japanese polka dot yarn to create a fashion ornament lightweight enough for three-season wear.

FINISHED MEASUREMENTS
42 x 10"/106.5 x 25.5cm

MATERIALS
Yarn A: 92yd/84m eyelash or fur yarn in green
Yarn B: 92yd/84m polka dot or confetti on carrier thread in black on black
Knitting needles: 12mm (size 17 U.S.), wood or bamboo recommended, *or size to obtain gauge*

GAUGE
5¼ sts and 10 rows = 4"/10cm with A and B tog in Garter Stitch
Always take time to check your gauge.

INSTRUCTIONS
Note: Yarns A and B are worked together throughout the pattern.

With A and B, CO 3 sts.

Row 1: K1inc1, k to last st, k1inc1—5 sts.
Rep row 1, inc on both sides until 55 sts, or until all the yarn is used. BO and cut yarn. Weave in ends.

THIS PROJECT WAS KNIT WITH
A 4 balls of Habu Textiles' A-27 *Poly Moire*, 100% polyester, 0.5oz/14g = approx 23yd/21m per ball, color #8 Wakakusa
B 2 balls of Habu Textiles' A-29 *Tobi Moire*, 100% polyester, 0.5oz/14g = approx 68yd/62m per ball, color #90 Black

A

B

ALTERNATE
This photo shows the project knit with Crystal Palace's *Splash*, 100% polyester, color Picnic, and Trendsetter's *Flora*, 76% viscose/24% polyester, color #1000 Black

Quicksilver
Collar

DESIGN BY
IRIS SCHREIER

SKILL LEVEL
◆ ◆ ◆ ◆

Easy

Everyone will want one of these sweet and airy all-weather adornments. This little wisp of a muffler is great for dressing up a plain suit or a tight-fitting tee. It's quick as can be to knit and perfect as a gift. For a fuller, more elaborate look, knit two of them in contrasting or complementary colors, such as gold and silver, and then twist the pair together.

FINISHED MEASUREMENTS
27 x 10"/68.5 x 25.5cm in Garter Stitch

MATERIALS
84yd/77m eyelash or fur yarn in silver
Knitting needles: 8mm (size 11 U.S.) bamboo circular needle *or size to obtain gauge*

GAUGE
10 sts and 12 rows = 4"/10cm in Garter Stitch
Always take time to check your gauge.

INSTRUCTIONS
CO 3 sts.

Row 1: K1inc1, k1inc1, k1inc1—6 sts
Row 2: K1inc1, k1inc1, k to last st, k1inc1—9 sts.
Rep row 2 (inc twice on one side and once on the other) until scarf measures 10"/25.5cm in length.

BO loosely. Cut yarn and weave in ends.

THIS PROJECT WAS KNIT WITH
1 ball of Trendsetter's *Perla*, 100% polyester, 0.7oz/20g = approx 84yd/77m, in color #53 Grey

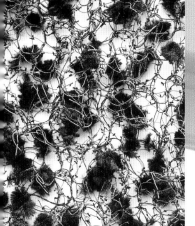

Filigree
Shawl

DESIGN BY
LAURIE KIMMELSTIEL

SKILL LEVEL
◆ ◆ ◇ ◇

Easy

Like a web of tiny leaves, this incredibly soft wrap doesn't look knitted at all. The simple Garter Stitch pattern uses two unique Japanese fibers to create a lace motif with very large needles (we recommend birch or bamboo). The resulting fabric has a wonderful stretchy, gauzy feel. If you've had some experience knitting with either very thin fibers or other exotic ones, this project is a breeze.

FINISHED MEASUREMENTS
Shawl: 54 x 18"/137 x 46cm

MATERIALS
Yarn A: 120yd/110m filigree yarn in brown
Yarn B: 120yd/110m polka dot on carrier thread in black
Knitting needles: 12mm (size 17 U.S.), wood or bamboo recommended, *or size to obtain gauge*

GAUGE
5 sts and 10 rows = 4"/10cm with A and B in Garter Stitch
Always take time to check your gauge.

INSTRUCTIONS
Note: Yarns A and B are worked together throughout.

With A and B, CO 3 sts.
Row 1: K1inc1, k to last st, k1inc1—5 sts.
Rep row 1 (inc at the beg and end of each row) until only sufficient yarn to BO remains. BO. Weave in ends.

THIS PROJECT WAS KNIT WITH
A   2 balls of Habu Textiles' *A-28 Kasumi*, 100% polyester, 0.5oz/14g = approx 60yd/55m per ball, color #5 Brown
B   2 balls of Habu Textiles' *A-29 Tobi Moire*, 100% polyester, 0.5oz/14g = approx 68yd/62m per ball, color #90 Black

A

B

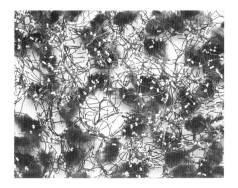

ALTERNATE
This photo shows the project knit with Habu Textiles' *A-28 Kasumi*, 100% polyester, color #90 Black and *A-29 Tobi Moire*, color #2 Enji

Black Tie Wrap

DESIGN BY
LAURIE KIMMELSTIEL

SKILL LEVEL
◆ ◆ ◆ ◆

Easy

I knitted this scarf while spending a few days at the Peters Valley Crafts Center in New Jersey, and it was a hit with potters as well as fiber artists, men and women alike. This triangular scarf looks most dramatic and interesting when worn in a way that shows off its open, wispy design. And although the yarns have very unusual textures, they rarely become knotted. Be sure to practice knitting with them before you begin the project itself.

Finished Measurements
36 x 14"/91.5 x 35.5cm

Materials
Yarn A: 43yd/39m confetti on carrier thread in black
Yarn B: 60yd/55m filigree yarn in black

Knitting needles: 12mm (size 17 U.S.), wood or bamboo recommended, *or size to obtain gauge*

Gauge
6 sts and 7 rows = 4"/10cm in Garter Stitch
Always take time to check your gauge.

Instructions
Note: Yarns A and B are worked together throughout until the last 3 or 4 rows, when B is worked alone.

With A and B, CO 3 sts.
Row 1: K1inc1, k to end—4 sts.

Rep row 1, inc at beg of each row, until all of yarn A has been used. Secure A by knotting its end to B. Cont to rep row 1 with B alone for 3 or 4 rows. BO loosely and cut yarn. Weave in ends.

This project was knit with
A 1 ball of Habu Textiles' *A-107 Feather Moire*, 83% polyester/17% nylon, 1oz/28g = approx 43yd/39m, color Black
B 1 ball of Habu Textiles' *A-28 Kasumi*, 100% polyester, 0.5oz/14g = approx 60yd/55m, color #10 Black

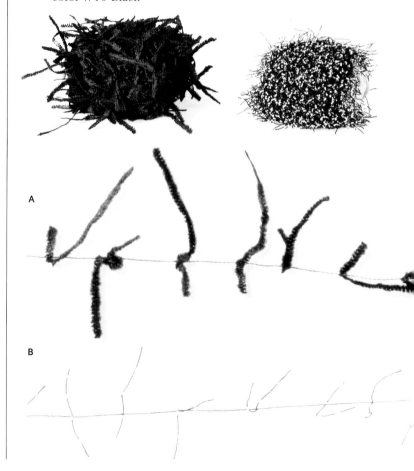

A

B

SILK

Silk is the glistening jewel of the textile trade, the ultimate luxury yarn

and the chosen fiber of royalty for centuries. It provides incomparable

drape and elegance and has a shimmering hand. In its purest form this

positively slinky and even crunchy material is extremely strong but can

be a challenge to knit with because of the lack of resiliency. It's best

to knit pure silk yarn tightly on smaller needles than used normally with

other yarns. With this in mind, most of the designs we've created here

use silk blends that show the thread at its maximum beauty but are

easier to knit.

Instant Karma Muffler

DESIGN BY
IRIS SCHREIER

SKILL LEVEL
◆ ◆ ◆ ◆

Beginner

It's extraordinary how a simple, soft muffler can make you feel harmonious with nature and in touch with your inner self… or not. But you'll love the way this scarf swings while you walk and makes you feel totally feminine. Make sure to wear it over your coat so that the pretty bouclé trim shows.

Finished Measurements
70 x 4"/178 x 10cm

Materials
Yarn A: 250yd/229m of light worsted weight silk or silk blend variegated yarn in plum
Yarn B: 50yd/45m of worsted weight wool bouclé in green
Knitting needles: 5.5mm (size 9 U.S.) *or size to obtain gauge*

Gauge
26 sts and 20 rows = 4"/10cm in Rib Stitch
Always take time to check your gauge.

Instructions
Note: The Yarn B trim is used only for the beginning and end of the scarf and requires only knit stitches. Each strand is worked alone.

With B, CO 26 sts.

Bottom Trim
Rows 1–4: K.
Cut B. Attach A.

Scarf Body
Row 5: K1, p1 across.
Rep row 5 until scarf measures 70"/175cm or desired length.

Top Trim
Attach B and cut A.
Rep rows 1–4.
BO all sts. Cut B and weave in all ends.

This project was knit with
A   1 hank of Great Adirondack's *Nassau*, 50% cotton/50% silk, light worsted weight, approx 315yd/288m, color Plum Loco
B   1 ball of Habu Textiles' *A-31 BF Ring*, 89% wool, worsted weight, 1 oz/28g = approx 50yd/45m, color #13 Green

A

B

Soho
Scarf

DESIGN BY
IRIS SCHREIER

SKILL LEVEL
♦ ♦ ♦ ♦
Intermediate

For a New Yorker like me, this scarf brings to mind the eclectic streets of Soho. Sleek and elegant as its namesake, this neck piece has two outer panels that are knit vertically, and the center panel is knit horizontally. This design is relatively easy to execute for those with some knitting experience.

FINISHED MEASUREMENTS
80 x 4½"/253 x 11cm

MATERIALS
Approx 200yd/183m silk or silk blend worsted weight yarn in variegated green
Knitting needles: 5mm (size 8 U.S.) 24"/60cm or longer circular needle *or size to obtain gauge*

GAUGE
10 sts and 26 rows = 4"/10cm in Garter Stitch
Always take time to check your gauge.

INSTRUCTIONS
Note: Knitting is continuous, except for the stitches that you'll pick up on the edge of the horizontal panel to complete the final vertical panel. The "p1, turn, s1" edging creates a series of looped stitches to make it easy to pick up stitches along one edge of the horizontal panel.

FIRST VERTICAL-KNIT PANEL
CO 200 sts.
Rows 1–10: K.

HORIZONTAL-KNIT PANEL
Row 1: CO an additional 6 sts—206 sts total—using the Knitted Cast On technique explained on page 22; turn.
Row 2: K5, skp; turn.
Row 3: S1, k4, p1; turn.
Row 4: S1, k4, skp; turn.

Rep rows 3–4 until 7 sts rem.
BO all sts, leaving last st on needle.

SECOND VERTICAL-KNIT PANEL
Pick up 199 sts along side of horizontal panel—total 200 sts. Make sure you insert needle under both loops of each edge st to pull through yarn as you create new sts.
P across these sts and continue purling until you have completed 10 rows.
BO all sts. Cut yarn and weave in ends.

THIS PROJECT WAS KNIT WITH
1 hank of Tess's *Cultivated Silk*, 100% silk, worsted weight, 3.5oz/100g = approx 200yd/183m, color Eucalyptus

ALTERNATE
This photo shows the project knit with Lorna's Laces' *Lion and Lamb* silk/wool blend, color #403 Tuscany

Scalloped Aegean Scarf

DESIGN BY
IRIS SCHREIER

SKILL LEVEL
◆ ◆ ◆

Intermediate

Exotically delicate and reminiscent of fresh sea breezes, this reversible scarf uses a double-knitting technique, with intricate lace panels separating its subtle stripes. Best knitted up with your most beautiful silk, this scarf looks great with two yarns of similar hues and can be comfortable in nearly any climate.

FINISHED MEASUREMENTS
78 x 7"/198 x 18cm

MATERIALS
Approx total: 640yd/584m silk or silk blend superfine weight yarn
Color A: 320yd/292m in pale aqua
Color B: 320yd/292m in turquoise
Knitting needles: 5mm (size 8 U.S.) *or size to obtain gauge*

GAUGE
26 sts and 24 rows = 4"/10cm in Stockinette Stitch
Always take time to check your gauge.

INSTRUCTIONS
Note: The pattern is worked throughout using 1 strand A and 1 strand B. A and B strands are knitted together when the instructions specify AB, and knitted and purled separately when instructions specify only A or only B. When knitting A or B separately take both colors to the back, and when purling A or B separately take both colors to the front. If this is your first time using this technique, please refer to the Double-Knit Pattern technique on page 18.

CO 45 sts with AB.
Row 1: K3 AB, *(k1 A, p1 B) 3 times, (with AB, k2tog, yo, k1, yo, skp) 1 time; rep from * to last 3 sts, k3 AB—45 sts
Row 2: K3 AB, *(k1 B, p1 A) 3 times, p5 AB; rep from * to last 3 sts, k3 AB—45 sts
Rep rows 1 and 2 until desired length.

BO with AB, k the knit sts and p the purl sts. Cut yarns and weave in ends.

THIS PROJECT WAS KNIT WITH
A 2 balls of Filatura di Crosa's/Tahki Stacy Charles's *Luxury,* 100% silk, fingering weight, 1.75oz/50g = approx 160yd/146m per ball, color #1
B 2 balls of Filatura di Crosa's/Tahki Stacy Charles's *Luxury,* 100% silk, fingering weight, 1.75oz/50g = approx 160yd/146m per ball, color #22

A

B

ALTERNATE
This photo shows the project knit with Anny Blatt Kanpur's *Pure Reeled Silk,* colors Cirrus #17 and Vitamine #609

North Cape Balaclava

DESIGN BY
LAURIE KIMMELSTIEL

SKILL LEVEL
◆ ◆ ◇ ◇

Easy

Need to spice up your winter look? This dramatic fashion garment serves as both a head covering and a scarf. It's long enough to circle your face and gently grace your neck and shoulders—a modern version of an Old World design that offers sophistication and panache. Knitted in the round on a set of large circular needles, our balaclava requires no complicated finishing. This is a great knitting project for a knitter on the go.

FINISHED MEASUREMENTS

16"/40.5cm long x 16⅛"/41cm circumference at top and 17¼"/43cm circumference at bottom

MATERIALS

Approx total: 572yd/523m silk or silk blend medium weight yarn
Color A: 286yd/262m in blue
Color B: 286yd/262m in maroon
Knitting needles: 9mm (size 13 U.S.) 16"/40.5cm circular needle *or size to obtain gauge*
Stitch marker

GAUGE

7½ sts and 16 rows = 4"/10cm with both A and B in Stockinette Stitch
Always take time to check your gauge.

INSTRUCTIONS

Note: The pattern is worked in the round throughout using one strand of A and one strand of B together. Make sure that the cast-on stitches haven't been twisted prior to starting round 1, so that the tube of fabric will be created properly.

BOTTOM SECTION

With A and B tog, CO 56 sts. Pm on right needle. Beg knitting in the round by inserting right needle into 1st CO st on left needle and knitting it, making sure sts aren't twisted. Cont k around until the piece measures 12"/30cm in length.

DECORATIVE BAND

Rnds 1–3: P around to marker.
Rnds 4–6: K around to marker.
Rnds 7–9: P around to marker.

TOP SECTION

Cont using k sts only until the piece measures 16"/41cm.
Begin dec as foll:
Rnd 1: *K5, k2tog; rep from * 7 more times—48 sts.
Rnds 2–6: K around to marker.
BO all sts, cut yarn, and weave in ends.

THIS PROJECT WAS KNIT WITH

A 2 balls of Lang's *Baccara,* 85% silk/15% nylon, worsted weight, 1.75oz/50g = approx 143yd/131m per ball, color Blue 0033

B 2 balls of Lang's *Baccara,* 85% silk/15% nylon, worsted weight, 1.75oz/50g = approx 143yd/131m per ball, color Maroon 0080

A

B

lattice

We discovered lattice's special quality when we began knitting with it and received raves about the drape and design of the resulting garments.

Two styles of lattice yarns are included in this category. In one, thin strands are joined at regular intervals by square flags (like a ladder with square rungs). The other, with confetti-like flags on a carrier thread, is slightly easier to knit with.

Lattice yarns don't need complicated stitches or exotic patterns to look beautiful, but they can be a challenge because you can easily pick up the wrong strand with your knitting needle. However, with minimal practice you can master these fibers, and the results are well worth your efforts. If you've never knitted with them before, consider making a practice swatch until you feel comfortable embarking on the patterns found in this chapter.

Lattice yarns may be knitted alone or in combination with carrier yarns such as the polka dot, sequin, and pom-pom yarns shown here. They knit up exquisitely into delicate-looking fabrics that are actually quite resilient and a pleasure to wear. To soften the piece, wash the finished accessory by hand in cold water prior to wearing it.

Flowing Diamonds Shawl

DESIGN BY
LAURIE KIMMELSTIEL

SKILL LEVEL
◆ ◆ ◇ ◇
Easy

Remarkably lightweight, this unusual shawl has a drape as fluid as light on water. The knitted fibers glisten, resembling thousands of tiny pieces of brilliant color. The diamond shape can be folded in half to form a triangle and worn like a kerchief, criss-crossing the tails to tie them behind your head. It's definitely a necessary accessory, and a versatile one at that.

FINISHED MEASUREMENTS
54 x 40"/137 x 101.5cm

MATERIALS
330yd/302m metallic ladder yarn in aqua/purple
Knitting needles: 9mm (size 13 U.S.) circular bamboo needle *or size to obtain gauge*

GAUGE
8½ sts and 12 rows = 4"/10cm in Garter Stitch
Always take time to check your gauge; the yarn is very stretchy, so the measurements given are approximate.

INSTRUCTIONS
Note: The shawl is knitted into a diamond shape by starting at one point.

CO 3 sts.

BOTTOM HALF
Row 1: K1inc1, k to end.
Rep row 1 until 85 sts.

TOP HALF
Row 1: K2tog, k to end
Rep row 1 until 3 sts.
BO rem sts. Cut yarn and weave in ends.

THE PROJECT WAS KNIT WITH
2 balls of South West Trading Company's *Melody,* 65% rayon/35% nylon, 1.8oz/50g = approx 165yd/151m per ball, color 516 Intensity

ALTERNATE
This photo shows the project knit with Plymouth's *Eros,* 100% nylon, 1.8oz/50g = approx 165yd/151m, color #3246

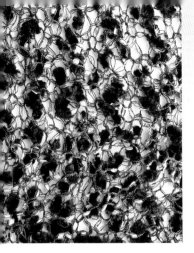

Bumblebee Shawl

DESIGN BY
LAURIE KIMMELSTIEL

SKILL LEVEL

◆ ◆ ◆ ◆

Easy

Like a swarm of honeybees, golden threads are striped with bits of black and gold and dotted with black pom-poms in this head-turning stole. This garment is so much fun to wear draped over bare shoulders. Onlookers will think those golden honey makers have encircled you.

FINISHED MEASUREMENTS
72 x 18"/183 x 46cm

MATERIALS
Yarn A: Approx 595yd/544m ladder yarn in black/gold
Yarn B: Approx 544yd/497m polka dot on carrier thread in black
Knitting needles: 12mm (size 17 U.S.) *or size to obtain gauge;* circular needle in nickel-plated brass for shawl body and bamboo recommended for trim

GAUGE
11 sts and 9 rows = 4"/10cm with A and B in Garter Stitch
Always take time to check your gauge.

INSTRUCTIONS
Note: This shawl is edged at each end with a narrow band of the ladder yarn. You may want to add fringe or fringed beads for an even more exotic look. A and B are knitted together, except for the first three and last three rows, where A is knitted alone. We recommend a circular needle because it's a slippery yarn project.

TOP TRIM
With A, loosely CO 50 sts with bamboo needle.
Rows 1–3: K.

SHAWL BODY
Attach B and, using A and B tog, k with nickel-plated circular needle.
Row 1: K.

Rep row 1 until piece measures 71"/180cm or to within 1"/2.5cm of desired length, making sure that at least 12yd/11m of the ladder yarn rem to complete the shawl. Cut B.

BOTTOM TRIM
Row 1: With A, k.
Rep row 1 a total of 3 times. BO loosely.
Cut yarn and weave in ends.

THIS PROJECT WAS KNIT WITH
A 4 balls of Plymouth's *Eros*, 100% nylon, ladder yarn, 1.8oz/50g = approx 165yd/151m per ball, color #4783
B 8 balls of Habu Textiles' *A-29 Tobi Moire*, polka dot on carrier thread, 100% polyester, 0.5oz/14g = 68yd/62m per ball, color Black

A

B

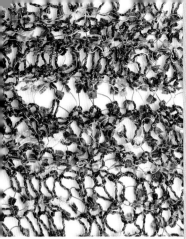

Trellis Stole

DESIGN BY
IRIS SCHREIER

SKILL LEVEL
◆ ◆ ◇ ◇

Easy

Can spring be far off
when you're wearing a
stole made to look like
tiny flowers that peek
through lacy lattice-
work? You'll find that
even though the fin-
ished piece looks elab-
orate, it's a quick and
very easy project (it's
knit lengthwise). The
pattern is so versatile
that you'll get decid-
edly different results
depending on the yarns
you choose. Combine
the confetti yarn with
cotton for a casual and
sturdier version, or use
a sparkly fiber for a
positively slinky look.

FINISHED MEASUREMENTS

75 x 13½"/191 x 34.5cm

MATERIALS

Yarn A: Approx 250yd/229m multicolored confetti on carrier thread

Yarn B: Approx 250yd/229m light cotton or synthetic lightweight yarn in teal

Knitting needles: 9mm (size 13 U.S.) *or size to obtain gauge;* wood or bamboo circular 29"/74.5cm or longer needle recommended

GAUGE

5 sts and 14 rows = 4"/10cm with A and B tog in Pattern Stitch

Always take time to check your gauge.

INSTRUCTIONS

Note: The project is worked with both A and B together, as well as separately, throughout. Don't cut the yarns when alternating them—just carry them over from one row to the next. Rows 24 and 25 form the center of the symmetrical pattern.

With A and B tog, CO 100 sts.

Rows 1–3: With A and B tog, k.

Row 4: With B, *k1, yo; rep from * to last st, k1.

Row 5: With B, *k1, dyo; rep from * to last st, k1.

Rows 6–7: With A, k.

Rows 8–15: Rep rows 4–7 twice.

Rows 16–17: With B, k.

Rows 18–19: With A, k.

Row 20: With A and B tog, *k1, yo; rep from * to last st, k1.

Row 21: With A and B tog, *k1, dyo; rep from * to last st, k1.

Rows 22–23: With B, k.

Row 24: With A, *k1, yo; rep from * to last st, k1.

Row 25: With A, *k1, dyo; rep from * to last st, k1.

Rows 26–27: With B, k.

Row 28: With A and B tog, *k1, yo; rep from * to last st, k1.

Row 29: With A and B tog, *k1, dyo; rep from * to last st, k1.

Rows 30–31: With A, k.

Rows 32–33: With B, k.

Rows 34–35: With A, k.

Row 36: With B, *k1, yo; rep from * to last st, k1.

Row 37: With B, *k1, dyo; rep from * to last st, k1.

Rows 38–45: Rep rows 34–37 twice.

Rows 46–48: With A and B tog, k.

BO all sts loosely. Cut A and B and weave in ends.

THIS PROJECT WAS KNIT WITH

A 4 balls Trendsetter's *Flora*, 76% viscose/24% polyamide confetti yarn, 1.8oz/50g = approx 70 yd/64m per ball, color Fall Leaves #166

B 3 balls Trendsetter's *Sunshine*, 74% viscose/25% polyamide, lightweight yarn, 1.8oz/50g = approx 95 yd/86m per ball, color #51 Dark Teal

A

B

ALTERNATE

This photo shows the project knit with S. Charles Collezione/Tahki Stacey Charles's *Cancun*, 68% polyester/8% cotton/10% polyamide/14% rayon confetti yarn, color #50, and Berroco's *Cotton Twist*, 70% mercerized cotton/30% rayon, light worsted weight, color #8307 Cactus Green

Gemstone
Scarf

DESIGN BY
LAURIE KIMMELSTIEL
AND IRIS SCHREIER

SKILL LEVEL
◆ ◆ ◇ ◇

Easy

If you could knit strands of precious stones, the result might look like this stunner. Large needles make it quick to knit, and the polka dot yarn embellishments give the ends of the piece just enough weight to make them swing as you move. So forget the usual necklace ... wear this unusual and delicate accessory instead.

FINISHED MEASUREMENTS
48 x 3"/122 x 7.5cm

MATERIALS
Yarn A: Approx 165yd/151m ladder yarn in red
Yarn B: Approx 68yd/62m polka dot on carrier thread in burgundy
Knitting needles: 9mm (size 13 U.S.) or *size to obtain gauge*; bamboo needles recommended for scarf body

GAUGE
27 sts and 12 rows = 4"/10cm with A in Garter Stitch
Always take time to check your gauge.

INSTRUCTIONS
Note: The project is worked with A and B together for the first six rows and the last six rows.

TOP TRIM
With A and B tog, CO 18 sts.
Rows 1–6: K.
Cut B.

BODY OF SCARF
Row 1: With A, k1, k1inc1, k to last 2 sts, k1inc1, k1—20 sts.
Row 2: K.
Rep row 2 until the piece measures 46"/117cm.

BOTTOM TRIM
Row 1: Add B and with A and B tog, k1, k2tog, k to last 3 sts, k2tog, k1—18 sts.
Rows 2–7: K.
BO all sts. Cut A and B, weave in ends.

THIS PROJECT WAS KNIT WITH
A 1 ball of Plymouth's *Eros*, 100% nylon, 1.8oz/50g = 165yd/151m, color Red #3260

B 1 ball of Habu Textiles' *A-29 Tobi Moire*, 100% polyester, 0.5oz/14g = 68yd/62m, color #2 Enji

A

B

MOHAIR
& angora

What we love most about mohair and angora yarns are their soft textures, warmth, and light weight. Used alone or spun with other fibers, mohair and angora, with their lustrous sheen, have a lot of give and superior loft. Both fibers are available in a wealth of beautiful colors. They also knit up relatively quickly. What follows here is a selection of our favorite mohair and angora patterns. Some are entirely mohair and others combine mohair or angora with other luxury fibers. These fibers are often imitated, so be on the lookout for the best-quality natural products for your knitted designs.

Romantic Ruffled Scarf

DESIGN BY
LAURIE KIMMELSTIEL

SKILL LEVEL
◆ ◆ ◇ ◇
Easy

Our frilly scarf is perfect for the knitter who wants to create something a bit exotic and still be able to complete a garment quickly and easily. This project has no complicated charts or confusing patterns to follow. Simple Garter Stitch and an easy yarn-over design show off this exquisite scarf with distinctive curly ribbon trim. Try knitting it using contrasting colors or experiment with various ribbons to create your own special border. Put on this soft scarf over a suit jacket or do the unexpected—wear it with a sweater and jeans.

FINISHED MEASUREMENTS
67 x 5"/170 x 13cm, including trim

MATERIALS
Yarn A: 370yd/338m mohair or mohair blend superfine weight yarn in pink
or 230yd/210m mohair or mohair blend lightweight yarn in pink
Yarn B: 20yd/18m curly ribbon tape or ½"/1.5cm flat ribbon in gray
Knitting needles: 5.5mm (size 9 U.S.) wood or bamboo needles *or size to obtain gauge*

GAUGE
18 sts and 20 rows = 4"/10cm in Garter Stitch
Always take time to check your gauge.

INSTRUCTIONS
Note: If you're knitting with superfine weight mohair, the project is worked with two strands throughout. For lightweight mohair, work it with a single strand.

With 1 or 2 strands of yarn A (see note), CO 24 sts.
Rows 1–3: K.
Row 4: *K1, yo; rep from * to last st, k1.
Row 5: *K1, dyo; rep from * to last st, k1.
Row 6: K.
Rep row 6 until the scarf measures 58"/147cm. Rep rows 4–5 and then rows 1–3. Loosely BO all sts on last row. Cut A.

BOTTOM TRIM
With Yarn B pick up 21 sts evenly across one end of scarf. If using curly ribbon tape, k 3 rows, being careful that the needle doesn't pierce the ribbon.
If using flat ribbon, work as follows:
Rows 1–3: K.
Row 4: *K1, yo; rep from * to last st, k1.
Row 5: *K1, dyo; rep from * to last st, k1.
Row 6: K.
BO all sts. Rep at other end of scarf. Cut yarn and weave in ends.

A

B

THIS PROJECT WAS KNIT WITH

A   2 balls of Habu Textiles' *A-32B Silk/Mohair,* 60% super kid mohair/40% silk, fingering weight, 0.5oz/14g = approx 185yd/169m per ball, color #32 Suo Pink

B   1 ball of Habu Textiles' *A-67 Fringe Tape,* 100% acetate, 1oz/28g = approx 20yd/18m, color #3 Gray

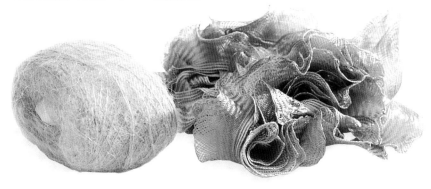

ALTERNATE

This photo shows the project knit with Fiesta's *Heaven,* 100% mohair, color Catalina, and Hanah's *Silk,* 100% silk, color Mossy Rock.

Basket
Weave
Muffler

DESIGN BY
LAURIE KIMMELSTIEL

SKILL LEVEL

◆ ◆ ◆ ◆

Easy

This classic scarf reminds me of a wool muffler my grandmother knitted more than half a century ago. The unique look relies on the traditional pattern but uses atypical colors, a nontraditional fiber, and extra length. The angora/wool blend eliminates the fuzziness of pure angora. The result is a very soft scarf that's a delight both to knit and to wear.

FINISHED MEASUREMENTS
84 x 6"/213 x 15cm

MATERIALS
Approx total: 492 yd/450m angora or angora blend medium weight yarn
Color A: 246yd/225m angora or angora blend medium weight yarn in olive
Color B: 246yd/225m angora or angora blend medium weight yarn in teal
Knitting needles: 5mm (size 8 U.S.) circular bamboo needle *or size to obtain gauge*

GAUGE
20 sts and 18 rows = 4"/10cm in Pattern Stitch
Always take time to check your gauge.

INSTRUCTIONS
Note: The project is knit with one strand throughout. Color A color block repeats four times and Color B color block repeats three times.

With yarn A, CO 30 sts.

Row 1: *K3, p3; rep from * 4 more times to end (total of 10 alternating "boxes").
Rows 2–3: Rep row 1.
Row 4: *P3, k3; rep from * 4 more times to end.
Rows 5–6: Rep row 4.
Rep rows 1–6 eight more times for a total of 54 rows, or 18 boxes. Cut A.

Attach B and rep as above to complete a 2nd section of 54 rows.
Cont knitting sections, alternating colors, to complete 7 sections (4 of A and 3 of B).
BO loosely and weave in ends.

THIS PROJECT WAS KNIT WITH
A 2 hanks of Classic Elite's *Lush,* 50% angora/ 50% wool, worsted weight, 1.8oz/50g = approx 123yd/112m per hank, color Olive Green #4497
B 2 hanks of Classic Elite's *Lush,* 50% angora/ 50% wool, worsted weight, 1.8oz/50g = approx 123yd/112m per hank, color Pale Teal #4472.

A

B

Je T'aime Cloche

DESIGN BY
LAURIE KIMMELSTIEL

SKILL LEVEL
◆ ◆ ◆ ◆

Intermediate

This yarn duo is a divine combination for a genuine cold-weather fashion statement. The rich color and luxurious texture of angora produce a wonderful and elegant hat knitted in a flapper-style design. Soft, loopy yarn frames your face with a narrow border that resembles tiny embroidered flowers. What could be more flattering, mon petit chou?

FINISHED MEASUREMENTS
16½ x 8"/42 x 20.5cm (before seams are sewn)

MATERIALS
Yarn A: 95yd/87m angora or angora blend medium weight yarn in blue
Yarn B: 44yd/40m rayon or rayon bouclé light-weight yarn in multicolor
Knitting needles: 4.25mm (size 6 U.S.) 16"/40.5cm circular needle *or size to obtain gauge*
4.25mm (size 6 U.S.) 6"/15cm double-pointed needles (set of 5) *or size to obtain gauge*
8 stitch markers
Tapestry needle

GAUGE
13½ sts and 32 rows = 4"/10cm in Stockinette Stitch
Always take time to check your gauge.

INSTRUCTIONS
Note: The main body of the hat is knitted in the round and the trim is knitted flat.

HAT TRIM
With B, tightly CO 68 sts with circular needle. Make sure to leave an 8–10"/20.5–25.5cm tail at beg of the CO edge to be able to sew tog the edge seam later.
Row 1: K.
Row 2: P.
Rep rows 1 and 2 one more time, or until piece measures ¾"/2cm.
Cut B.

HAT BODY
Attach A. With A, k to end, joining row and pm at join.
Rnd 1: K to marker.
Rep rnd 1 until hat measures 6¼"/16cm from bottom edge.

HAT TOP
Rnd 1: *K15, k2tog; rep from * 3 more times—64 sts.
Rnd 2: K.
Rnd 3: *K6, k2tog, pm; rep from *—56 sts.
Rnd 4: K.
Rnd 5: *K to 2 sts before marker, k2tog; rep from *.
Rnd 6: K.
Rep rnds 5–6 until 40 sts rem. Change to dpn. See the Transferring to Double-Pointed Needles from Circular Needle technique on page 18. Divide sts equally onto 4 dpn and continue to k

as follows, moving markers along as necessary. For instructions on placing markers on dpn, see page 18.

Rep rnds 5–6 until 16 sts rem.

Next rnd: * K2tog; rep from * to end of rnd— 8 sts.

Cut the yarn, leaving a 10–12"/25.5–31.5cm length; thread it through a tapestry needle. Insert tapestry needle through the 8 sts rem on your needles, drawing the yarn through these sts and gradually pulling them tog and off the needles to form a tiny circle at the top of the hat. Pull snugly but not too tightly and weave in the yarn. Turn the hat WS out and carefully sew the bouclé edge seam, using the leftover tail from beg of your CO. Weave in ends.

alternate

THIS PROJECT WAS KNIT WITH

A 3 balls of Joseph Galler Yarns' *Belangor,* 100% angora, worsted weight, 0.4oz/10g = approx 33yd/30m per ball, color #863 Copen Blue

B 1 ball of Muench Yarns' *Fabu,* 90% viscose/10% polyester, 1.8oz/50g, approx 79yd/72m, color #M4311 Blue/brown/olive

A

B

ALTERNATE

This photo shows the project knit with K1C2's *Douceur et Soie,* 70% mohair/30% silk, color #8532 Loden, Stahl's *Lambada,* 55% cotton/45% rayon, color #9655 Turmalin, and trimmed with Muench's *Fabu,* 90% rayon/10% polyester, color #M4311 Blue/brown/olive

Feathery Lace Stole

DESIGN BY
IRIS SCHREIER

SKILL LEVEL
◆ ◆ ◇ ◇

Easy

Airy, easy luxury describes this wisp of a stole. It's so versatile that you can tie it around your neck in winter or wear it as a lightweight shawl on a cool summer evening. Although it may appear to be a complicated knit, it won't need a lot of concentration, since the two-row stitch pattern is easy to memorize (which can't be said for many lace projects).

Finished Measurements
57 x 19"/145 x 48.5cm

Materials
460yd/421m mohair or mohair blend light-weight yarn in blue
Knitting needles: 5mm (size 8 U.S.) *or size to obtain gauge*

Gauge
16 sts and 21 rows = 4"/10cm in Pattern Stitch
Always take time to check your gauge.

Instructions
CO 75 sts.
Row 1: K3, *k2tog, yo, k1, yo, skp, k3; rep from * to end.
Row 2: K3, *p5, k3; rep from * to end.
Rep rows 1 and 2 until desired length. BO loosely. Cut yarn and weave in ends.

This project was knit with
2 balls of Rowan's *Kidsilk Haze,* 70% super kid mohair/30% silk, light worsted weight, 230yd/210m = approx 0.9oz/25g per ball, color #592 Heavenly

Barely
There
Scarf and
Wrap

DESIGN BY
IRIS SCHREIER

SKILL LEVEL
◆ ◆ ◆ ◆

Intermediate

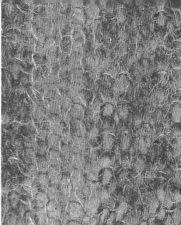

What a great excuse to wear a knitted piece in the summertime (as if you needed one). As a shawl this super-lightweight garment is fluffy-soft and luxurious—the perfect cover-up for a sleeveless outfit in summer. Yet the narrower scarf version will keep you luxuriously warm, even on the bitterest cold days. Either way, you'll barely notice you're wearing it. How to decide? Treat yourself... make both.

Choose a complementary pair of solid colors of mohair. The reversible pattern creates single-color vertical stripes (a different color on each side and a different stripe width in each piece) that alternate with two-strand Garter Stitch knitting.

SCARF

FINISHED MEASUREMENTS
64 x 5"/163 x 13cm

MATERIALS
Approx total: 460 yd/420m mohair or mohair blend lightweight yarn
Color A: 230yd/210m in red
Color B: 230yd/210m in orange
Knitting needles: 5.5mm (size 9 U.S.) *or size to obtain gauge*

GAUGE
24 sts and 18 rows = 4"/10cm using 2 strands in Pattern Stitch
Always take time to check your gauge.

INSTRUCTIONS
Note: The pattern is worked throughout using 1 strand A and 1 strand B. A and B strands are knitted together when the instructions specify AB, and knitted and purled separately when instructions specify only A or only B. When knitting A or B separately take both colors to the back, and when purling A or B separately take both colors to the front. If this is your first time using this technique, refer to the Double-Knit Pattern technique on page 18.

CO 30 sts with AB.

Row 1: *K3 AB, (k1 A, p1 B) 3 times; rep from * to last 3 sts, k3 AB—30 sts
Row 2: *K3 AB, (k1 B, p1 A) 3 times; rep from * to last 3 sts, k3 AB—30 sts

Rep rows 1 and 2 to desired length. BO using AB, k the knit sts and p the purl sts. Cut yarn, and weave in ends.

A

B

Wrap

Finished Measurements
56 x 11"/142 x 28cm

Materials
Approx total: 920yd/842m mohair or mohair blend lightweight yarn
Color A: 460yd/421m in red
Color B: 460yd/421m in orange
Knitting needles: 5.5mm (size 9 U.S.) *or size to obtain gauge*

Gauge
24 sts and 18 rows = 4"/10cm using 2 strands in Pattern Stitch
Always take time to check your gauge.

Instructions
See note for scarf, page 82.
Holding 2 strands tog (1 strand each of A and B), CO 66 sts.

Row 1: K6 AB, (k1 A, p1 B) 3 times, *k2 AB, (k1 B, p1 A) once, k2 AB, (k1 A, p1 B) 3 times; rep from * to last 6 sts, k6 AB—66 sts
Row 2: K6 AB, (k1 B, p1 A) 3 times, *k2 AB, (k1 A, p1 B) once, k2 AB, (k1 B, p1 A) 3 times; rep from * to last 6 sts, k6 AB—66 sts
Rep rows 1 and 2 to desired length. BO using AB, k the knit sts and p the purl sts. Cut yarn and weave in ends.

The projects were knit with
A 2 balls (4 balls for wrap) of Rowan's *Kidsilk Haze,* 70% super kid mohair/30% silk, light worsted weight, 230yd/210m = approx 0.9oz/25g per ball, color #606 Candy Girl

B 2 balls (4 balls for wrap) of Rowan's *Kidsilk Haze,* 70% super kid mohair/30% silk, light worsted weight, 230yd/210m = approx 0.9oz/25g per ball, color #596 Marmalade

A

B

suede

Imagine being able to create exotic and chic accessories with a faux fiber. The yarns used in this chapter are all faux suede, but they look and feel so authentic that you may have to convince non-leather-wearing friends that they can wear it guilt-free. We were delighted to discover the soft hand and flexibility of this unique fiber. We designed two belts and a purse that are especially suited to the incredible colors and firm nature of this leather-like material, yet you'll find that the finished pieces have lots of suppleness, and the yarn moves smoothly through your hands and needles.

Fringed Hippie Belt

DESIGN BY
IRIS SCHREIER

SKILL LEVEL

◆ ◆ ◇ ◇

Easy

This easy-to-make belt is a terrific accessory that looks great with almost any outfit. Because the two decorative fringes hanging from the rings are tied together to secure the belt, it can be resized to fit over any outfit and is perfect for all shapes and sizes. Feel free to wear it loosely around the waist, below the hips, or anywhere in between. Loop it through your favorite jeans or slip it loosely over a slim skirt. The swinging fringe will emphasize your every move to make you feel feminine and sexy. Check out your favorite notions shop for a pair of unusual or vintage belt rings and you'll be ready to go.

FINISHED MEASUREMENTS
33 x 2"/84 x 5cm, excluding fringe

MATERIALS
100yd/91m rayon or rayon blend faux suede yarn, multicolor
Knitting needles: 4.5mm (size 7 U.S.) *or size to obtain gauge*
Two 2"/5cm rings

GAUGE
20 sts and 18 rows = 4"/10cm in Pattern Stitch
Always take time to check your gauge.

INSTRUCTIONS
CO 8 sts onto 1st ring, according to detailed instructions on page 22, Casting On to a Belt Ring.

Row 1: K.
Row 2: K1inc1, k to end.
Row 3: K1inc1, k to end—10 sts.
Row 4: *K1, yo; rep from * to last st, k1.
Row 5: *K1, dyo; rep from * to last st, k1.
Rows 6–8: K.
Rep rows 4–8 until piece measures 31"/79cm, ending with row 5.

Next row: K2tog, k to end—9 sts.
Next row: K2tog, k to end—8 sts.

BO, attaching 2nd ring according to the instructions on page 23, Binding Off from a Belt Ring. Cut yarn. Weave in ends.

FRINGE
Cut twenty 38"/97cm strands of yarn. Each fringe will use 10 strands. Follow the instructions on page 19, Making Fringe, to attach a fringe to each of the two rings.

THIS PROJECT WAS KNIT WITH
2 skeins of Great Adirondack's *Suede,* 90% rayon/10% cotton suede yarn, approx 50yd/46m per skein, color Paprika

Hip Hugger Belt

DESIGN BY
LAURIE KIMMELSTIEL

SKILL LEVEL
◆ ◆ ◆ ◆

Easy

When we first saw this suede fiber (rayon, actually), Iris and I were stymied about how we should or could knit with it. I started experimenting with designs that illustrate my more unusual fashion sensibilities. Though you might want a subtler color scheme, consider the fun of wearing this one over basic black. I've sized it to fit average hips, but you can adjust it by either increasing or decreasing the overall length. Funky buttons add the final zing to this exciting and unexpected knitted accessory.

FINISHED MEASUREMENTS
41 x 4½"/104 x 11.5cm

MATERIALS
150yd/137m rayon or rayon blend faux suede yarn in multicolor
Knitting needles: 4.25mm (size 6 U.S.) *or size to obtain gauge*
Sewing needle and thread in contrasting color to attach buttons
3 square buttons, ¹¹⁄₁₆"/0.6cm

GAUGE
26 sts and 25 rows = 4"/10cm in Stockinette Stitch
Always take time to check your gauge.

INSTRUCTIONS
CO 3 sts.

Row 1: K.
Row 2: S1, k1inc1, k1—4 sts.
Row 3: S1, p1inc1, p1inc1, p1—6 sts.
Row 4: S1, k1inc1, k2, k1inc1, k1—8 sts.
Row 5: S1, p1inc1, p to last 2 sts, p1inc1, p1—10 sts.
Row 6: S1, k1inc1, k to last 2 sts, k1inc1, k1—12 sts.
Rep rows 5–6 until 26 sts or piece measures 4"/10cm.

DIAGONAL DESIGN
Row 1: K1inc1, k to end.

Row 2: P2tog, p to end.
Rep rows 1–2, ending with a p row, until piece measures 38"/96.5cm or desired hip measurement.

Begin buttonholes as foll:
Row 1: K3, yo, k10, yo, k10, yo, k3.
Row 2: P3, dyo, p10, dyo, p10, dyo, p3.
Row 3: K.
Row 4: P2tog, p to last 2 sts, p2tog—24 sts.
Row 5: K to last 3 sts, ssk, k1—23 sts.
Row 6: P2tog, p to end.
BO all sts. Cut yarn and weave in ends.
Using sewing thread and needle, sew on buttons, lining them up on the diagonal with the buttonholes.

THIS PROJECT WAS KNIT WITH
3 skeins of Great Adirondack's *Suede,* 90% rayon/10% cotton suede yarn, approx 50yd/46m per skein, color Rainbow

Back-to-the-Sixties Patchwork Bag

DESIGN BY
LAURIE KIMMELSTIEL

SKILL LEVEL
◆ ◆ ◆ ◆

Intermediate
(includes crochet)

What a great way to use leftover yarns! By simply alternating knitting and purling, you can create a patchwork of color and texture just like those real suede purses from the sixties. You could also easily knit this one in a single color or increase your palette to more colors. And while it's knitted here in a smaller version, the bag is still large enough to hold your keys and a cell phone (a reinforced bottom prevents sagging). Improvise and expand the size simply by increasing the number or size of patches, and don't forget to brush up on your single-crochet technique for the finishing touch.

Finished Measurements

5½ x 6¼"/14 x 16cm, excluding
crocheted edge

Materials

Approx total: 288yd/263m of suede yarn
Color A: 72yd/66m suede yarn in black
Color B: 72yd/66m suede yarn in blue violet
Color C: 72yd/66m suede yarn in green
Color D: 72yd/66m suede yarn in turquoise
Knitting needles: 3.25mm (size 3 U.S.) *or size to obtain gauge*
Pins for fastening seams
Small crochet hook
Corder for strap (optional)
Tapestry needle for fastening strap

Gauge

26 sts and 23 rows = 4"/10cm in Pattern Stitch
Always take time to check your gauge.

Instructions

Note: The purse is knit in one piece, and the sides are crocheted together. If you don't have a corder, you can braid
the yarn into a strap instead.

Pattern Stitch A

Row 1: K12, p12, k12.
Row 2: P12, k12, p12.
Rep rows 1–2 six more times for a total of 14 rows.

Pattern Stitch B

Row 1: P12, k12, p12.
Row 2: K12, p12, k12.
Rep rows 1–2 six more times for a total of 14 rows.

With A, CO 36 sts.

Side 1

Rows 1–2: With A, p. Cut A, attach B.
With B, follow rows 1–14 of Pattern Stitch A. Cut B,
attach A.
Rows 1–2: With A, p. Cut A, attach C.
With C, follow rows 1–14 of Pattern Stitch B. Cut C,
attach A.
Rows 1–2: With A, p. Cut A, attach D.
With D, follow rows 1–14 of Pattern Stitch A. Cut D,
attach A.
Rows 1–2: With A, p.

Reinforced Bottom

Attach 2nd strand of A. Using 2 strands of A tog,
Row 1: P.
Row 2: K.

Row 3: P.
Cut 1 strand of A and, using 1 strand of A alone,
Row 4: K. Cut A, attach B.

Side 2

With B, follow rows 1–14 of Pattern Stitch A. Cut B,
attach A.
Rows 1–2: With A, p. Cut A, attach C.
With C, follow rows 1–14 of Pattern Stitch B. Cut C,
attach A.
Rows 1–2: With A, p. Cut A, attach D.
With D, follow rows 1–14 of Pattern Stitch A. Cut D,
attach A.
Rows 1–2: With A, p.
BO all sts, and cut yarn.

Finishing

Fold piece in half and with WS tog, pin the outside edges.
Using small crochet hook and color A, single-crochet one
side's edges tog and then rep on other side of purse to
create an edge trim.

Strap

Cut 3 pieces of A, each approx 4yd/4m long. Knot the 3
pieces tog, 8"/20.5cm from each end. Following directions on corder, attach cut strands to corder and twist yarn
until the strap doubles onto itself. Knot on either end.
Thread tapestry needle with A. Sew strap to purse
1½"/4cm inside top edge at right and left. Alternatively,
you could cut 6 strands of color A, each approx 72"/2m
long, and braid these pieces. Knot on either end then
attach as above.

Weave in all loose ends.

This project was knit with

4 spools of Silk City
Viscose Suede, 50% vis-
cose/25% cotton/ 25%
polyester, approx
72yd/66m per spool,
colors 002 Black, 155
Blue Violet, 726 Cilantro,
and 096 Turquoise

A

B

C

D

RIBBON

Ribbon yarn isn't yarn in the true sense of the word—ribbon is woven,

not spun—so it lacks elasticity and can look a bit crunched when knit-

ted like other yarns. However, in this chapter you'll find projects that

take advantage of ribbon's best yarn qualities: a tightly knitted purse

made with an elasticized product that lets it stretch a bit, and a shawl

and scarves that use wrapping techniques that make the most of the

ribbon's flat surfaces. We've chosen a selection of the most extraor-

dinary ribbons, much like those we're sure you've coveted and stashed

away for years. We think you'll like the variety of designs and new

techniques explored here.

· · · · ·

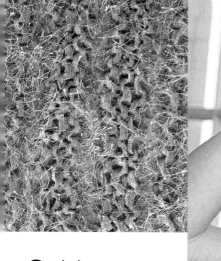

Golden Threads Boa

DESIGN BY
IRIS SCHREIER

SKILL LEVEL

◆ ◆ ◆ ◆

Easy

Although it bears an uncanny resemblance to a wooly caterpillar's fur, this stole doesn't require any transformation to get rave reviews. The ribbon and eyelash yarns each have a unique multifaceted texture, and together they create a garment that feels bouncy, almost spongy. It's surprisingly lightweight, considering how much yarn is used to construct it. Wear it like a boa or wrap it around your neck for warmth like a wide scarf. You could even drape it over your shoulders, perhaps using a favorite pin to fasten the ends.

FINISHED MEASUREMENTS
58 x 12½"/147 x 32cm

MATERIALS
Yarn A: 200yd/183m ribbon yarn in aqua
Yarn B: 92yd/84m eyelash or fur yarn in beige
Knitting needles: 9mm (size 13 U.S.)
32"/81.5cm or longer circular needle *or size to obtain gauge*

GAUGE
12 sts and 16 rows = 4"/10cm in Garter Stitch
Always take time to check your gauge.

INSTRUCTIONS
Note: The stole is knit vertically. A and B are used separately throughout but never cut. Instead, the yarn is carried over from one row to the next.

With A, CO 170 sts.

Rows 1–4: With A, k—4 rows.
Rows 5–6: With B, k—2 rows.
Rows 7–10: With A, k—4 rows.
Rows 11–12: With B, k—2 rows.
Rows 13–14: With A, k—2 rows.
Rows 15–16: With B, k—2 rows.
Rows 17–20: With A, k—4 rows.
Rows 21–22: With B, k—2 rows.
Rows 23–28: With A, k—6 rows.
Rows 29–30: With B, k—2 rows.
Rows 31–34: With A, k—4 rows.
Rows 35–36: With B, k—2 rows.
Rows 37–38: With A, k—2 rows.
Rows 39–40: With B, k—2 rows.
Rows 41–44: With A, k—4 rows.

Rows 45–46: With B, k —2 rows.
Rows 47–50: With A, k—4 rows.
BO all sts. Cut yarn and weave in ends.

THIS PROJECT WAS KNIT WITH
A 2 balls of Gedifra's *Poesie,* 40% nylon/32% polyester/28% microfiber ribbon yarn, 1.8oz/50g = approx 99yd/91m per ball, color #2017

B 4 balls of Habu Textiles' *A-27 Poly Moire,* 100% polyester eyelash yarn, 0.5oz/14g = approx 23yd/21m per ball, color 24 Beige

A

B

Dazzling
Hair
Circlet

DESIGN BY
LAURIE KIMMELSTIEL

SKILL LEVEL

◆ ◆ ◆ ◆

Easy

Headbands are no longer just for little girls; they've become chic accessories for sophisticated women. I whipped up this one with a crinkly, stretchy ribbon and a thin metallic yarn.

FINISHED MEASUREMENTS
2 x 14½"/5 x 37cm

MATERIALS
Yarn A: 50yd/46m crinkly ribbon yarn in black
Yarn B: 50yd/46m metallic superfine weight yarn in copper
Knitting needles: 5mm (size 8 U.S.) 16"/40.5cm circular needle *or size to obtain gauge;* wood or bamboo recommended
Stitch marker

GAUGE
15½ sts and 40 rows = 4"/10cm with A and B together in Garter Stitch
Always take time to check your gauge.

INSTRUCTIONS
Note: Yarns A and B are worked together throughout.

With A and B, CO 56 sts, pm, join yarns, and begin knitting in the round as foll:

Rnds 1–4: K to marker.
Rnds 5–8: P to marker.
Rnds 9–12: Rep rnds 1–4.
Rnds 13–16: Rep rnds 5–8.
Rnds 17–20: Rep rnds 1–4.

BO very, very loosely. Cut yarn, weave in ends.

THIS PROJECT WAS KNIT WITH
A 1 ball of Lang *Passione,* 50% rayon/46% nylon/4% Elastan ribbon yarn, 1.8oz/50gr = approx 130yd/119m, color #0004 Black
B 1 ball of Rowan *Lurex Shimmer,* 80% viscose/20% polyester superfine yarn, 0.9oz/25gr = approx 104yd/95m, color #330 Copper

A

B

Ribbon-Wrapped Scarf and Shawl

DESIGN BY
IRIS SCHREIER

SKILL LEVEL
◆ ◆ ◆ ◆
Intermediate

Here's a different way to use delicate ribbons in your knitting. The special technique found in this pattern will have you weaving along with your knitting. The result is an exquisite garment that doesn't look knitted. The scarf and shawl have outstanding drape. This is a perfect project for fragile ribbons whose beauty and character might be obscured by traditional knitted stitches.

FINISHED MEASUREMENTS

78 x 4"/198 x 10cm for scarf
57 x 12"/145 x 30.5cm for shawl

MATERIALS

Scarf
Yarn A: 164yd/150m silk or silk blend light worsted weight yarn in lilac
Yarn B: 100yd/91m ¼"/6mm silk ribbon in gray/purple
Shawl
Yarn A: 246yd/225m silk or silk blend light worsted weight yarn in light green
Yarn B: 164yd/150m ¼"/6mm silk ribbon in light green/dark green
Knitting needles: 9mm (size 13 U.S.) *or size to obtain gauge*

GAUGE

11 sts and 9 rows = 4"/10cm in Pattern Stitch
Always take time to check your gauge.

INSTRUCTIONS

Note: Throughout this project you'll knit with A and weave with B. To ensure that B doesn't become twisted and tightened, slacken the ribbon by stretching out each row after it's completed. Refer to the Ribbon Wrapping instructions on page 21 to review this technique.

With A, CO 11 sts for scarf (33 sts for shawl). Attach B.
Rows 1–5: With A, p1. *Bring B to front, and with A, k1. Passing B over st just knitted, bring B to back and with A, p1. Rep from * to end.
Row 6: With A, p1. Bring B to front. *With A, yo, k1. Passing B over st just knitted, bring B to back and with A, yo, p1. Passing B behind st just purled, bring B to front. Rep from * to end.
Row 7: With A, p1. Bring B to front. *With A, dyo, k1. Passing B over st just knitted, bring B to back and with A, dyo, p1. Passing B behind st just purled, bring B to front. Rep from * to end.
Rep rows 1–7 a total of 3 times.
Rep rows 1–5 until scarf measures 65"/165cm (shawl 56"/142cm) or desired length. End as foll:
Row 1: With A, p1. Bring B to front. *With A, yo, k1. Passing B over st just knitted, bring B to back and with A, yo, p1. Passing B behind st just purled, bring B to front. Rep from * to end.
Row 2: With A, p1. Bring B to front. *With A, dyo, k1. Passing B over st just knitted, bring B to back and with A, dyo, p1. Passing B behind st just purled, bring B to front. Rep from * to end.
Rows 3–7: With A, p1. *Bring B to front, and with A, k1. Passing B over st just knitted, bring B to back and with A, p1. Rep from * to end.
Rep rows 1–7 a total of 3 times. BO sts. Cut yarn. Weave in ends.

THE SCARF WAS KNIT WITH

A 2 hanks of Classic Elite's *Interlude,* 70% linen/30% silk worsted weight yarn, 1.8oz/50g = approx 82yd/75m per hank, color #20286 Lilac Ice

B 1 hank of Classic Elite's *Playful Weekend,* 100% silk ¼"/6mm ribbon, 1.8oz/50g = approx 355yd/325m, color #50018 Sapphire

THE SHAWL WAS KNIT WITH

A 3 hanks of Classic Elite's *Interlude,* 70% linen/30% silk worsted weight yarn, 1.8oz/50g = approx 82yd/75m per hank, color #20272 Citron

B 1 hank of Classic Elite's *Playful Weekend,* 100% silk 1/4"/6mm ribbon, 1.8oz/50g = approx 355yd/325m, color #50021 Tourmaline

ALTERNATE

This photo shows the project knit with Great Adirondack's Irisee *Shell,* 95% rayon/5% polyester, color Plum Loco, and Treenway's *Bombyx* 20/10, 100% silk, color 210 Berry Blaze.

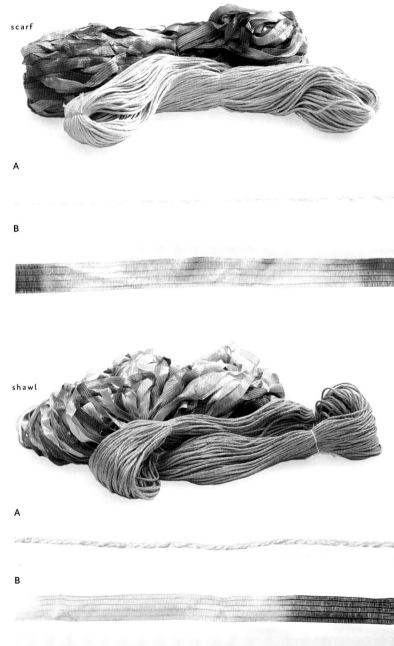

scarf

A

B

shawl

A

B

Enchanting Fur Hat

DESIGN BY
LAURIE KIMMELSTIEL

SKILL LEVEL
◆ ◆ ◆

Intermediate

Lush metallic yarn, knit with deep Chinese-red ribbon yarn and circled with a trim of quirky fur, makes this snug hat a wardrobe standout. Would you believe it, I got accolades on the subway while knitting it? And even though it uses four yarns and three sets of needles, you'll find that it's a pretty straightforward pattern after all.

FINISHED MEASUREMENTS
15 x 8"/38 x 20.5cm

MATERIALS
Yarn A: 5yd/5m cotton or cotton blend light worsted yarn in black
Yarn B: 120yd/110m polyester or rayon fur yarn in black
Yarn C: 82yd/75m nylon or nylon blend worsted weight metallic yarn in gold
Yarn D: 75yd/69m rayon or rayon blend ribbon in red
Knitting needles: 5.5mm (size 9 U.S.) 16"/40.5cm circular needle, for knitting fur trim
6mm (size 10 U.S.) 16"/40.5cm circular needle *or size to obtain gauge,* for hat body and band around edge
6mm (size 10 U.S.) set of double-pointed needles 6"/15cm long *or size to obtain gauge,* for top of hat
Stitch marker
Tapestry needle

GAUGE
15 sts and 20 rows = 4"/10cm in Stockinette Stitch on size 10 U.S. needles with C and D together
Always take time to check your gauge.

INSTRUCTIONS
Note: For A use one strand. For B use two strands together. C and D are knitted together throughout using one strand of each. You'll be changing from circular to double-pointed needles halfway through the project. See page 18 for more information about this technique. In order to get a snug fit, a knitted band of cotton yarn goes under the very stretchy fur trim. You may need to use a smaller needle size for the fur.

HAT BAND
With A and 6mm circular needle, CO 56 sts.
Row 1: P.

FUR TRIM
Cut A, attach 2 strands B, and change to 5.5mm circular needle. Pm at beg of row, join sts, and cont to k around.
Rnd 1: With B, k to marker.
Rnd 2: K9, k2tog, *k7, k2tog; rep from * 4 more times across row—50 sts.
Rnd 3: K to marker.
Rep rnd 3 until piece measures at least 3"/7.5cm. Cut B.

HAT BODY
Attach C and D and change to 6mm circular needle.
Rnd 1: With C and D, k9, k1inc1, *k7, k1inc1; rep from * 4 more times across rnd—56 sts.
Rnd 2: K to marker.
Rep rnd 2 until piece measures at least 6"/15cm.

HAT TOP

Rnd 1: *K5, k2tog; rep from * to marker—48 sts.

Rnd 2: K to marker.

Rnd 3: *K4, k2tog; rep from * to marker—40 sts.

Rnd 4: K to marker.

Rnd 5: *K3, k2tog; rep from * to marker—32 sts. Change to dpn and evenly distribute sts equally among 3 or 4 needles. Cont to mark the beg of each row with a st marker.

Rnd 6: K to marker.

Rnd 7: *K2, k2tog; rep from * to marker—24 sts.

Rnd 8: K to marker.

Rnd 9: *K1, k2tog; rep from * to marker—16 sts.

Rnd 10: K to marker.

Rnd 11: *K2tog; rep from * to marker—8 sts.

Cut yarn, leaving a 12"/30.5cm tail, and thread it through tapestry needle. Insert tapestry needle through rem 8 sts on needles. Pull through all 8 st loops and tighten snugly to close top of hat, then carefully remove needles and weave in end at top of hat to secure. Cut yarn. Sew bottom edge seam tog and secure by weaving in all loose ends.

THIS PROJECT WAS KNIT WITH

A 1 ball of S. Charles Collezione/Tahki Stacey Charles's *Victoria,* 60% cotton/40% viscose, lightweight worsted, 1.8oz/50g = approx 70yd/64m, color #12 Black

B 2 balls of Lion Brand's *Fun Fur,* 100% polyester fur yarn, 1.8oz/50g = approx 60yd/55m per ball, color #153 Black

C 1 skein of Berroco's *Quest,* 100% nylon, worsted weight, 1.8oz/50g = approx 82yd/75m, color Antique Gold #9824

D 1 skein of Berroco's *Glacé,* 100% rayon ribbon yarn, 1.8oz/50g = approx 75yd/69m, color Cool Red #2655

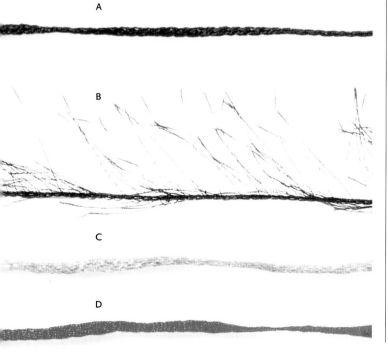

A

B

C

D

Victorian Purse

DESIGN BY
LAURIE KIMMELSTIEL

SKILL LEVEL
◆ ◆ ◆ ◆

Intermediate

We're often inspired to copy styles from bygone days, and this Victorian purse embodies both the elegance of another era and the concept of unexpected knitwear. This project's remarkable elasticity, unique shape, and striking appearance bring together all that we love about luxury ribbon. The sweet little handbag has a special rolled edging, a corded ribbon handle, and a beaded tassel; its pretty details will add sparkle to a special night out.

FINISHED MEASUREMENTS
7½ x 5"/19 x 13cm, excluding tassel

MATERIALS
Yarn A: 170yd/155m metallic medium weight ribbon in gold/black
Yarn B: 75yd/69m rayon or rayon blend ribbon for trim in black
Yarn C: 10yd/9m silk superfine yarn for tassel in black
Knitting needles: 3.5mm (size 4 U.S.) circular or straight needles *or size to obtain gauge*
3.5mm (size 4 U.S.) double-pointed needles *or size to obtain gauge*
6 stitch markers
Tapestry needle
32 fire-polish metallic beads, 4mm each, for tassel
Corder for twisting ribbon for purse handle (optional)
Sewing needle and thread for adding beads to tassel
Crochet hook

GAUGE
23 sts and 28 rows = 4"/10cm in Stockinette Stitch
Always take time to check your gauge.

INSTRUCTIONS
Note: For more information about moving stitches from circular to double-pointed needles, see page 18.

With A and circular or straight needle, CO 60 sts. Change to dpn and divide evenly among them (15 sts on each of 4 dpn or 20 sts on each of 3

dpn). Pm, join, and k in the round.

TOP OF PURSE
Rnd 1: K to marker.
Rep rnd 1 until piece measures 2½"/6.5cm.

DECORATIVE TRIM
Rnds 1–3: With A, p to marker.
Drop A (but don't cut), attach B.
Rnds 4–5: With B, k to marker.
Rnds 6–7: With A, p to marker.
Rnds 8–9: With B, k to marker. Cut B, leaving sufficient yarn to secure and weave in ends.
Rnds 10–12: With A, p to marker.

PURSE BODY
Rnd 1: With A, k to marker.
Rep rnd 1 until piece measures 5"/13cm.

PURSE BOTTOM
Begin dec as foll:
Rnd 1: With A, *k8, k2tog, pm; rep from * to last 10 sts, k8, k2tog—54 sts.
Rnds 2–4: K.
Rnd 5: *K to 2 sts before marker, k2tog; rep from * to last 2 sts, k2tog.
Rep rnds 2–5 until 6 sts rem.

Cut A, leaving 10"/25.5cm tail. Thread tapestry needle with A, insert tapestry needle through rem 6 sts, and pull tightly to close purse bottom. Knot tail to secure.

BEADED TASSEL
Cut fifteen 12"/30.5cm strands of C
Cut one 16"/40.5cm strand of C

Using crochet hook, pull strap from one inside corner of purse to outside, slipping the end under the rolled edge of purse. Knot the strap a minimum of 4 or 5 times to ensure that it's secure, then trim it to hide the end. Repeat on other side.

Weave in all loose ends.

THIS PROJECT WAS KNIT WITH

A   2 hanks of Berroco's *Metallic FX,* 85% rayon/15% metallic worsted weight chained ribbon, 0.8oz/25g = approx 85yd/78m per hank, color Black & Gold #1003

B   1 hank of Berroco's *Glacé,* 100% rayon light worsted weight ribbon, 1.8oz/50g = approx 75yd/69m, color Black #2012

C   1 spool of Halcyon's *Gemstone Silk* Item 158 2/12, 100% silk, fingering weight, 105yd/96m, color Black #14

Create tassel as described on page 20. Attach the tassel between the center 2 sts of the bound-off sts at the bottom of the purse.

Add 1 bead to each of the 32 strands of the tassel, tying them close to the bottom of the strands, according to the instructions on page 21.

PURSE STRAP

The purse strap can be twisted with a corder or braided by hand.

If using a corder, cut 2 pieces of A, each approx 5yd/6m. Knot the 2 pieces about 2"/5cm from each end. Follow the directions for the corder and twist the yarn until it doubles onto itself. For the braid, cut 3 pieces of A, approximately 2.5yd/2.25m each. Knot on one end and braid to desired length. Knot on the other side to secure braid.

A

B

C

Mermaid's Tail Evening Bag

DESIGN BY
LAURIE KIMMELSTIEL

SKILL LEVEL
◆ ◆ ◆ ◆

Intermediate

The dangling strands of ribbon attached to the fishtail bottom of this delicate, shiny knitted purse will wriggle along as you move. We love the collaboration of stretchy knitted ribbon fabric and smooth glistening fringe. You'll find this roomy little handbag quite simple to make and fun to wear.

FINISHED MEASUREMENTS

7½ x 6½"/19 x 16.5cm, in Stockinette Stitch; width measured at base

MATERIALS

184yd/168m ¼"/6mm multicolored shiny ribbon
Knitting needles: 3.5mm (size 4 U.S.) *or size to obtain gauge*
Medium crochet hook
Pins for fastening seams
Tapestry needle for sewing seams
Corder for twisting ribbon for purse strap or 2 dpns 3.5mm (size 4 U.S.) for I-cord strap method

GAUGE

19 sts and 27 rows = 4"/10cm in Stockinette Stitch
Always take time to check your gauge.

INSTRUCTIONS

Note: This purse is knitted from the top of one side down to the bottom, then back up to the top of the other side.

CO 28 sts.
Rows 1–5: K.
Row 6: K.
Row 7: P.
Rep rows 6–7 until piece measures 5¾"/15cm, ending with a p row.

INCREASE BOTTOM

Row 1: *K1inc1, k8; rep from * 2 more times, k1inc1—32 sts.
Row 2: P.
Row 3: *K1inc1, k9, k1inc1, k10, k1inc1, k9, k1inc1—36 sts.
Row 4: P.
Row 5: K1inc1, k10, *k1inc1, k11; rep from * once, k1inc1—40 sts.
Rows 6–7: P.
Rows 8, 10, 12, 14: K.
Rows 9, 11, 13, 15: P.
Row 16: P.

DECREASE FOR BODY

Row 17: K2tog, k10, k2tog, k11, k2tog, k11, k2tog—36 sts.
Row 18: P.
Row 19: K2tog, k9, k2tog, k9, k2tog, k10, k2tog—32 sts.
Row 20: P.
Row 21: *K2tog, k8; rep from * 2 more times, k2tog—28 sts.

Cont as foll:
Row 1: K.
Row 2: P.
Rep rows 1–2 until piece measures 13"/33cm, ending with a p row.

ENDING

Rows 1–5: K.
BO loosely. Cut yarn and weave in ends.

Gently press completed piece with a warm iron. Fold piece in half, WS tog, and pin. Thread tapestry needle with yarn; stitch piece together and turn inside out.

STRAP

The strap can be twisted with a corder or knitted into an I-cord.

If using a corder, cut 3 pieces of yarn, each approx 4¼ yd/4m long. Knot the 3 pieces 8"/20.5cm from each end. Follow the directions for the corder and twist the yarn until cord doubles onto itself. Cut 3 pieces of yarn, each 18"/46cm. Fold in half and slip through folded end of cord. Slip this yarn through its loop to secure to end of cord so that each end of cord now has 6 ribbons hanging from knots at each end. To secure the cord to the corners of the purse, pull the knotted end through the seamed edge of purse (strap will stay in place with knot on outside of seams). Rep with other end of strap on opposite edge of purse. Weave in all loose ends.

If making an I-cord, with dpn, leave an 8"/20.5cm tail and CO 2 sts. *K 1 row. Without turning your work, slip the sts back toward the other end of the needle. Pull the yarn snugly and begin knitting again. Repeat from * until cord is desired length. BO, making sure to leave an 8"/20.5cm tail of ribbon at end of cord. With crochet hook, pull one end of I-cord through seamed edge of purse. *Cut 3 pieces of yarn, each 18"/46cm. Fold these in half and, with crochet hook, slip this folded loop of yarn through end st of I-cord. Slip all ends of yarn (there will be 7 total, including tail attached to end of I-cord) through the folded tail to knot. Pull these down snugly to tighten and then knot once or twice to secure strap in place. With crochet hook, pull other end of I-cord through opposite side of purse and repeat from *. Trim ends to even lengths. Weave in all loose ends.

THIS PROJECT WAS KNIT WITH

2 balls of Muench's *Venezia*, 93% rayon/7% nylon ribbon yarn, 1.8oz/50gm = approx 92yd/84m per ball, color #4 Green/brown/multi

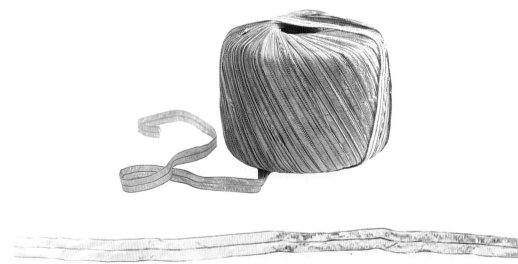

wool

Ah, wool. After handling extravagant and elegant luxury wool, you'll never again think of it as a homely, scratchy fiber that should be relegated to a third-grade coatroom. Certain breeds of sheep produce exceptional fleece, and the resulting spun fibers are known for their uniformity, density, and fineness. A fine hand in wool may be hard to find, but once you've experienced such knitting, you'll know true love. The following projects represent our journey through these lush fibers, rich color palettes, and unexpected shapes and patterns.

· · · ·

"Hat for All" Rolled Cap

DESIGN BY
LAURIE KIMMELSTIEL

SKILL LEVEL

◆ ◆ ◇ ◇

Easy

This basic unisex hat has been in my design repertoire for many years, yet it always draws raves for its chic style and wonderful comfort and warmth. Try knitting it with almost any medium weight wool. Experiment with both solid and striped hats too. Dress it up or down. Knit up a whole series of hats for all the special people in your life.

FINISHED MEASUREMENTS

20 x 8"/51 x 20.5cm
(before seams are sewn)

MATERIALS

Approx total: 240yd/219m wool or wool blend DK weight yarn
Color A: 1.8oz/50g = 120yd/110m in lime
Color B: 1.8oz/50g = 120yd/110m in olive
Knitting needles: 6mm (size 10 U.S.) *or size to obtain gauge*
Tapestry needle
Pins for fastening seam

GAUGE

13 sts and 21 rows = 4"/10cm in Stockinette Stitch using 2 strands tog
Always take time to check your gauge.

INSTRUCTIONS

Note: Use two strands together, one of each color, throughout. The hat is knitted in one flat piece then seamed together.

With A and B, CO 64 sts.
Row 1: K.
Row 2: P.
Rep rows 1–2 until piece measures at least 5.5"/14cm. Feel free to adjust the height, depending on whether you want a longer or shorter hat.

Begin dec as foll:
Row 1: *K6, k2tog; rep from * to end—56 sts.
Row 2 and all even rows: P.
Row 3: *K5, k2tog; rep from * to end—48 sts.
Row 5: *K4, k2tog; rep from * to end—40 sts.
Row 7: *K3, k2tog; rep from * to end—32 sts.

Row 9: *K2, k2tog; rep from * to end—24 sts.
Row 11: *K1, k2tog; rep from * to end—16 sts.
Row 13: *K2tog; rep from * to end—8 sts.

Cut yarn, leaving 24"/61cm tail. Thread yarn on tapestry needle and pass tapestry needle through rem 8 sts. Pull yarn through to tighten these sts. Leave tapestry needle threaded. Fold hat with RS facing and pin seam evenly. Using the tapestry needle that is still threaded with rem yarn, and beg at top of hat, sew tog at edges, being careful to reverse sewing side on last 1½"/4cm of knitted fabric for rolled-up brim. Weave in ends. Turn hat RS out.

THIS PROJECT WAS KNIT WITH

A   1 ball of Debbie Bliss's Merino DK, 100% wool, DK weight, 1.8oz/50g = approx 120yd/110m, color Soft Lime #225501

B   1 ball of Debbie Bliss's Merino DK, 100% wool, DK weight, 1.8oz/50g = approx 120yd/110m, color Bright Olive #225502

A

B

Big Blocks Scarf

DESIGN BY
LAURIE KIMMELSTIEL

SKILL LEVEL

◆ ◆ ◇ ◇

Easy

This scarf's motif reminds us of a toddler's wooden alphabet blocks. It's a speedy project that's bright, cheery, and ideal for a new knitter. I chose a type of yarn with distinctive texture that's unusual for standard worsted weight yarns. Extra length gives the scarf a funky, youthful style.

FINISHED MEASUREMENTS
70 x 6"/178 x 15cm

MATERIALS
Approx total: 390yd/357m wool or wool blend worsted weight yarn
Color A: 130yd/119m in light green
Color B: 130yd/119m in purple
Color C: 130yd/119m in yellow
Knitting needles: 6mm (size 10 U.S.) circular needle preferred *or size to obtain gauge*
Tapestry needle to weave in ends

GAUGE
14 sts and 24 rows = 4"/10cm in Garter Stitch
Always take time to check your gauge.

INSTRUCTIONS
Note: The scarf has a right, or front, side for clarity in the pattern instructions only. A stripe of color in the first row of a color change indicates the wrong, or back, side. For a clean, crisp design, be sure that you change colors on the same side with each new block.

With A, CO 22 sts.

BOTTOM EDGE
Row 1 (RS): With A, k.
Row 2: K.
Row 3: P.
Row 4: P.

FIRST BLOCK
Rows 1–32: With A, k.
Rows 33–34: P.
Cut A and attach B on RS.

SECOND BLOCK
Rows 1–32: With B, k.
Rows 33–34: P.
Cut B and attach C on RS.

THIRD BLOCK
Rows 1–32: With C, k.
Rows 33–34: P.
Cut C and attach A on RS.

Rep 1st through 3rd blocks in the color order of A, B, C 3 more times, until 12 blocks are complete.

TOP EDGE (foll last 2 rows of p)
Rows 1–2: With C, k.
BO all sts, cut yarn, and weave in ends.

THIS PROJECT WAS KNIT WITH
A 2 balls of Classic Elite's *Bazic,* 100% superwash wool, medium worsted weight, 1.8oz/50g = approx 65yd/59m per ball, color #2902

B 2 balls of Classic Elite's *Bazic,* 100% superwash wool, medium worsted weight, 1.8oz/50g = approx 65yd/59m per ball, color #2925

C 2 balls of Classic Elite's *Bazic,* 100% superwash wool, medium worsted weight, 1.8oz/50g = approx 65yd/59m per ball, color #2995

A

B

C

Super-Bulky
Collar Lapel

DESIGN BY
LAURIE KIMMELSTIEL

SKILL LEVEL
◆ ◆ ◆ ◆

Intermediate

I love quirky super-bulky yarn. It's soft enough to snuggle around your neck, but the spun fiber's diameter is so large that the scarf design demands to be rather innovative to compensate for the weight of the yarn. This lapel falls just where it's needed most and doesn't double back on itself, so there's no extra volume to weigh you down.

FINISHED MEASUREMENTS
18"/46cm x 6"/15cm
along each of 4 panels

MATERIALS
Approx 132yd/121m wool or wool blend bulky yarn in red
Knitting needles: 12mm (size 17 U.S.) 10"/25.5cm wooden straight needles recommended *or size to obtain gauge*

GAUGE
8 sts and 14 rows = 4"/10cm in Garter Stitch

INSTRUCTIONS
CO 2 sts.

Row 1: K.
Row 2: K1inc1, k1inc1—4 sts.
Row 3: K.
Row 4: K1inc1, k to last st, k1inc1.
Rep rows 3–4 until 16 sts wide.

SECTION 1
Row 1: K1inc1, k to last st—17 sts.
Row 2: K2tog, k to last st—16 sts.
Rep rows 1–2 until piece measures 18"/46cm from beg.

SECTION 2
Row 1: K2tog, k to last st.
Row 2: K1inc1, k to last st.
Rep rows 1–2 until piece measures 18"/46cm from top corner of previous diagonal piece (see diagram).

SECTION 3
Row 1: K1inc1, k to last st.
Row 2: K2tog, k to last st.
Rep rows 1–2 until piece measures 18"/46cm from top corner of previous diagonal piece.

SECTION 4
Row 1: K2tog, k to last st.
Row 2: K1inc1, k to last st.
Rep rows 1–2 until piece measures 14"/35.5cm from corner of previous diagonal piece, making sure to end with row 1—16 sts.

END OF SCARF
Row 1: K2tog, k to end—15 sts.
Row 2: K1inc1, k to last 2 sts, k2tog—15 sts.
Row 3: K2tog, k to end—14 sts.
Row 4: K1inc1, k to last 2 sts, k2tog—14 sts.
Row 5: K2tog, k to end—13 sts.
Row 6: BO 1st 10 sts, k to end.
Row 7: BO rem 3 sts. Cut yarn and weave in ends.

THIS PROJECT WAS KNIT WITH
1 skein of Brown Sheep's *Burly Spun Wool*, 100% wool, bulky weight, 8oz/227g = approx 132yd/121m, color Prairie Fire #BS181

Hot & Now
Scarf

DESIGN BY
IRIS SCHREIER

SKILL LEVEL
◆ ◆ ◇ ◇

Easy

This sleek scarf is fun to knit because of its numerous colors. Choose a single color and pick close shades of yarn or experiment with completely different colors. Swatch them to ensure that you're positioning the colors in the most attractive order. The rows are knit lengthwise to achieve vertical striping, and the entire piece requires fewer than 30 rows of knitting. So here's a great project for novice knitters once they've managed to cast on all those stitches! Use soft merino wool that you enjoy knitting with, and you'll find the design so straightforward that you'll probably finish it in one sitting.

FINISHED MEASUREMENTS
60 x 4"/152 x 10cm, excluding fringe

MATERIALS
Approx total: 392yd/358m wool or wool blend light worsted weight yarn
Color A: 98yd/90m in red
Color B: 98yd/90m in pink
Color C: 98yd/90m in orange
Color D: 98yd/90m in fuchsia
Knitting needles: 9mm (size 13 U.S.) 40"/101.5cm or longer circular needle *or size to obtain gauge*
Medium or large crochet hook for attaching fringes

GAUGE
12 sts and 24 rows = 4"/10cm in Garter Stitch using 2 strands tog
Always take time to check your gauge.

INSTRUCTIONS
Note: Hold together one end from the inside of the ball of yarn and one end from the outside of it. Knit using two strands of a single color throughout.

With 2 strands of A, CO 180 sts.

Rows 1–5: K.
Cut both strands of A, leaving 2 hanging 6"/15cm strands.
Attach 2 strands of B.
Rows 6–11: With B, k.
Cut both strands of B, leaving 2 hanging 6"/15cm strands.
Attach 2 strands of C.
Rows 12–17: With C, k.
Cut both strands of C, leaving 2 hanging 6"/15cm strands.
Attach 2 strands of D.
Rows 18–22: With D, k.
Row 23: With D, BO all sts loosely.
Cut both strands of D, leaving 2 hanging 6"/15cm strands.

FRINGE (make 6 for each side)
Cut twelve 12"/30cm lengths of A, B, C, and D, for a total of 48 pieces. Each fringe uses 4 strands, 1 each of A, B, C, and D.

Space 6 fringes evenly along each side of the scarf. Follow the instructions on page 19 for making fringe. Wherever there are hanging strands as specified above, include those when you create the fringe by pulling those through the loop. For a more even look, omit the extra lengths of those colors that are already hanging. Trim ends evenly.

A

B

C

D

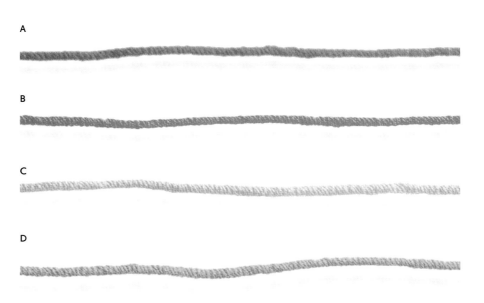

Honey
Bear
Hat

DESIGN BY
LAURIE KIMMELSTIEL

SKILL LEVEL
◆ ◆ ◆ ◆

Intermediate

Outdoorsy style and a rich color scheme make this fabulous hat a standout. Not only does it look terrific on every head, but also the combination of fibers makes it very soft and a real joy to wear. The design may look a bit difficult, but in fact, it's a relatively simple pattern. And since the hat is knitted in sections, each part can be increased or decreased in length to suit the size of the wearer's head. It has a comfortable fit, and because it's seamless, there is no finishing necessary when you complete your knitting.

FINISHED MEASUREMENTS
17½ x 17"/44.5 x 22cm (before seams are sewn)

MATERIALS
Yarn A: 98yd/90m wool or wool blend light weight yarn in orange
Yarn B: 98yd/90m rayon or silk blend lightweight yarn in multicolor

Knitting needles: 6.5mm (size 10½ U.S.) 16"/40.5cm circular needle *or size to obtain gauge*
6.5mm (size 10½ U.S.) double-pointed needles (set of 5) *or size to obtain gauge*
Stitch marker
Tapestry needle

GAUGE
12½ sts and 20 rows = 4"/10cm in Stockinette Stitch
Always take time to check your gauge.

INSTRUCTIONS
Note: Yarns A and B are worked together throughout.

BOTTOM
Holding both strands tog, CO 55 sts onto circular needle. Join to form a circle and pm here to indicate the end of the rnd.
Rnd 1: K.
Rep rnd 1 until piece measures 2¼"/6cm.

MIDDLE
Rnd 1: K1, *p1, k1; rep from * to end.
Rnd 2: P1, *k1, p1; rep from * to end.
Rep rnds 1–2 until piece measures 5½"/14cm.
Next rnd: K1inc1, k to end—56 sts.
Next rnd: K.

Top

Beg dec as foll:

Rnd 1: *K6, k2tog, rep from * to end—49 sts.

Rnd 2: K.

Rnd 3: *K5, k2tog; rep from * to end—42 sts.

Rnd 4: K.

Rnd 5: *K4, k2tog; rep from * to end—35 sts.

Transfer sts to 4 dpn, dividing sts among the needles (9, 9, 9, 8) and using the 5th needle to continue the knitting. For more information, see Transferring to Double-Pointed Needles from Circular Needles on page 18.

Rnd 6: K.

Rnd 7: K.

Rnd 8: *K3, k2tog; rep from * to end—28 sts.

Rnds 9–10: K.

Rnd 11: * K2, k2tog; rep from * to end—21 sts.

Rnd 12: K.

Rnd 13: *K1, k2tog; rep from * to end—14 sts.

Rnd 14: K.

Rnd 15: *K2tog; rep from * to end—7 sts.

Cut A and B, leaving 10"/25.5cm tail. Thread both A and B through a tapestry needle and insert it through the remaining 7 sts, gradually pulling these sts off the dpn and gathering the top of the hat. Pull tight, but not taut, to close the circle at the top of the hat, and weave this thread into the crown of the hat. Weave in ends.

THIS PROJECT WAS KNIT WITH

A 1 ball of Karabella Yarn's *Aurora 8,* 100% merino wool, light worsted weight, 1.8oz/50g = approx 98yd/90m, color #704

B Partial skein of Blue Heron's *Beaded Rayon,* 100% rayon, dk weight, 8oz/227g = approx 525yd/480m per skein, color Daffodil

A

B

Flying V Scarf

DESIGN BY
IRIS SCHREIER

SKILL LEVEL
◆ ◆ ◆ ◆
Intermediate

Variegated yarns are beautiful when knit on the diagonal. No two variegates are the same, either; compare the two very different motifs that emerge in the main project and in the alternate one. This piece has a lovely symmetry—diagonals intersect in the center. Although the beginning of the scarf will require your special attention, you'll find that once the first few rows are set up, it's completely effortless knitting.

FINISHED MEASUREMENTS
65 x 5"/165 x 13cm

MATERIALS
Approx total: 200yd/183m wool or wool blend medium weight yarn in variegated, pink/green
Knitting needles: 5.5mm (size 9 U.S.) *or size to obtain gauge*

GAUGE
18 sts and 26 rows = 4"/10cm in Garter Stitch
Always take time to check your gauge.

INSTRUCTIONS
CO 17 sts.

SCARF BOTTOM
Row 1: K1inc1, k1; turn—leave 15 sts unknitted.
Row 2: S1, k2; turn.
Row 3: K1inc1, k3; turn—leave 14 sts unknitted.
Row 4: S1, k4; turn.
Row 5: K1inc1, k5; turn—leave 13 sts unknitted.
Row 6: S1, k6; turn.
Row 7: K1inc1, k7; turn—leave 12 sts unknitted.
Row 8: S1, k8; turn.
Row 9: K1inc1, k9; turn—leave 11 sts unknitted.
Row 10: S1, k10; turn.
Row 11: K1inc1, k11; turn—leave 10 sts unknitted.
Row 12: S1, k12; turn.
Row 13: K1inc1, k13; turn—leave 9 sts unknitted.
Row 14: S1, k14; turn.
Row 15: K1inc1, k23—25 sts.
On the other side, rep rows 1–14 to create another triangle on the straight sts.

SCARF MIDDLE
Row 1: K1inc1, k14, skp, k15—32 sts.
Rep row 1 to desired length.

FINISHING
Row 1: Skp, k13, skp, k14, s1.
Row 2: Skp, k13, skp, k12, s1.

Row 3: Skp, k11, skp, k12, s1.
Row 4: Skp, k11, skp, k10, s1.
Row 5: Skp, k9, skp, k10, s1.
Row 6: Skp, k9, skp, k8, s1.
Row 7: Skp, k7, skp, k8, s1.
Row 8: Skp, k7, skp, k6, s1.
Row 9: Skp, k5, skp, k6, s1.
Row 10: Skp, k5, skp, k4, s1.
Row 11: Skp, k3, skp, k4, s1.
Row 12: Skp, k3, skp, k2, s1.
Row 13: Skp, k1, skp, k2, s1.
Row 14: Skp, k1, skp, s1.
Row 15: Skp, BO rem sts.
Cut yarn. Weave in ends.

THIS PROJECT WAS KNIT WITH
1 skein of Artyarns' *Modular Wool/Silk,* 50% merino wool/50% silk, worsted weight, 4oz/113g = approx 280yd/256m, color Tokyo Lily

ALTERNATE
This photo shows the project knit with 2 balls of Filatura Di Crosa's *127 Print,* 100% wool, color #20 Red

SEQUINS

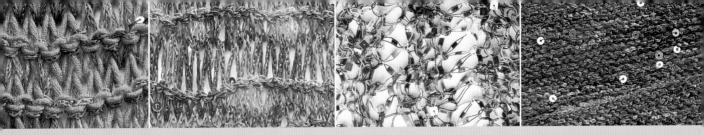

Like jewels on a string, these very special yarns add a sparkling new dimension to any knitting project. We discovered sequin yarns and their unique qualities while searching for fibers that could add excitement and elegance to simpler ones such as cotton and silk. Sequin yarns are perfect for evening-wear accessories; the sequins look like tiny jewels knit into the shimmering pieces presented here. We love the look of tassels on the sequin scarves so much that we designed two versions, a narrow one for warm weather or indoor wear and a wider one suitable for colder weather.

Swing Scarf

DESIGN BY
IRIS SCHREIER

SKILL LEVEL
◆ ◆ ◆ ◆

Easy

This lovely dual-textured scarf combines delicate sequined yarn with a glossy cotton (though silk would work just as well). The second fiber gives this lovely lacelike piece enough substance and warmth to make it an all-weather accessory, and at the same time makes it slightly easier to knit the slippery sequin yarn. Try using it as a belt, wrapping it several times around your waist for a fun and colorful look. The pattern is easy to follow, and you'll enjoy adding pretty beads and sequins to your tassels for a dressy look.

FINISHED MEASUREMENTS
76 x 3"/203 x 8cm, not including tassels

MATERIALS
Yarn A: 100yd/92m variegated fine weight sequin yarn in plum
Yarn B: 100yd/92m glossy fine weight cotton or silk yarn in deep pink
Knitting needles: 10mm (size 15 U.S.) *or size to obtain gauge*
Sequins or beads (optional)
Sewing needle and thread (optional) for attaching beads to tassels
Small and large crochet hooks for attaching tassels

GAUGE
20 sts and 9 rows = 4"/10cm in Garter Stitch
Always take time to check your gauge.

INSTRUCTIONS
With A and B tog, CO 3 sts.

BOTTOM BORDER
Row 1: K1inc1, k to end—4 sts.
Rep row 1 eleven times (inc at the beginning of each row) until 15 sts.

SCARF BODY
Row 1: K.
Rep row 1 until scarf measures 70"/178cm or desired length.

TOP BORDER
Dec for next 12 rows as foll:
Row 1: K2tog, k to end—14 sts.
Rep row 1 eleven times (dec at the beginning of each row) until 3 sts.
BO rem 3 sts and cut yarn after passing it through last st. Weave in ends.

Use the method described on page 20 to add tassels. If you'd like to add sequins or beads to the tassels, follow the directions on page 21.

THIS PROJECT WAS KNIT WITH
A 1 hank of Great Adirondack's *Holographic Sequins,* 90% rayon/10% polyester, approx 100yd/92m, color Plum Loco
B 1 ball of Rowan's *Cotton Glacé,* 100% cotton, 1.8oz/50g, approx 137yd/125m, color Bubbles #724

A

B

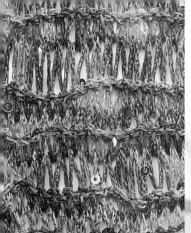

Opera
Scarf

DESIGN BY
LAURIE KIMMELSTIEL

SKILL LEVEL
◆ ◆ ◆ ◆
Intermediate

This lightweight and narrow silk-tasseled scarf is strung with beautiful beads for added pizzazz. Wear it like a long colorful necklace. I knitted this one on a flight from San Francisco to New York—the flight crew and passengers were very excited about the project. (Half the fun was answering their questions about what I was knitting.) The quick-to-knit piece has a bit of a lacy design that adds interest to an already exquisite yarn.

FINISHED MEASUREMENTS
65 x 3"/163 x 8cm, not including tassels

MATERIALS
Yarn A: 100yd/91m variegated fine weight sequin yarn in multicolor
Yarn B: 5yd/5m superfine silk yarn for tassels in orange
Knitting Needles: 6.5mm (size 10½ U.S.) bamboo needles *or size to obtain gauge*
Sewing needle and thread for adding beads or sequins to tassels (optional)
Sequins or beads for tassels (optional)
Small and large crochet hooks for attaching tassels

GAUGE
19 sts and 12 rows = 4"/10cm in Pattern Stitch
Always take time to check your gauge

INSTRUCTIONS
CO 3 sts.

BOTTOM BORDER
Row 1: K1inc1, k remaining sts to end—4 sts.
Rep row 1 ten times (inc at the beginning of each row) until 14 sts.

SCARF BODY
Row 1: *K1, yo; rep from * to last st; k1.
Row 2: *K1, dyo; rep from * to last st; k1.
Rows 3–5: K.
Row 6: * K1, yo; rep from * to last st; k1.
Row 7: *K1, dyo; rep from * to last st; k1.
Rows 8–9: K.
Rep rows 1–9 until scarf measures 55"/115cm from the beg, or desired length, before dec border; leave sufficient yarn for completion and tassels. Measure carefully on a flat surface; don't stretch scarf.

TOP BORDER
Row 1: K2tog, k to end—13 sts.
Rep row 1 until 3 sts.
BO rem 3 sts and cut yarn after passing it through last st. Weave in ends.

TASSELS
Make 2 as foll:
Cut ten 10"/25cm lengths of A
Cut two 15"/38cm lengths of B
Cut ten 10"/25cm lengths of B

Use half of the 10"/25cm strands of sequin and silk yarn and 1 of the 15"/38cm lengths of silk yarn for one tassel. Follow the instructions on page 20 for Making Tassels. Rep on other end of scarf with rem strands of tassel yarn.

For a more glittery effect, attach sequins to the tassels, following the instructions on page 21 for Attaching Beads or Sequins to Tassels.

THIS PROJECT WAS KNIT WITH
A 1 hank of Great Adirondack's *Holographic Sequins,* 90% rayon/10% polyester, approx 100yd/92m, color Tourmaline
B 1 minicone of Halcyon's *2/12 Gemstone Silk,* 100% silk, fingering weight, approx 105yd/96m, color #5 Nectarine

A

B

Jeweled Scarf

DESIGN BY
IRIS SCHREIER

SKILL LEVEL
◆ ◆ ◆ ◆

Intermediate

Imagine a scarf that can be worn like a beautiful piece of jewelry! You can instantly dress up any outfit with this exquisite collaboration of sequins and ladder yarn. Try it out with various color combinations too. This little scarf knits up very quickly into a semicircular shape that will comfortably and gracefully encircle your neck.

FINISHED MEASUREMENTS
35 x 10"/89 x 25cm, not including fringe

MATERIALS
Yarn A: 100yd/91m ladder yarn in light brown/dark brown
Yarn B: 100yd/91m gold sequins on black carrier thread
Knitting needles: 9mm (Size 13 U.S.) needles *or size to obtain gauge*
Large crochet hook for attaching fringe

GAUGE
9 sts and 14 rows = 4"/10cm in Pattern Stitch
Always take time to check your gauge.

INSTRUCTIONS
Note: Yarns A and B are knit together throughout.

SCARF BODY
Using A and B tog, CO 3 sts.
Row 1: K1inc1, k1inc1, k1inc1—6 sts.
Rows 2–7: K1inc1, k1inc1, k to last st, k1inc1—24 sts.
Row 8: *K1, yo; rep from * to last st, k1.
Row 9: *K1, dyo; rep from * to last st, k1.
Rows 10–14: K1inc1, k1inc1, k to last st, k1inc1—39 sts.
Row 15: *K1, yo; rep from * to last st, k1.
Row 16: *K1, dyo; rep from * to last st, k1.
Rows 17–21: K1inc1, k1inc1, k to last st, k1inc1—54 sts.
Row 22: *K1, yo; rep from * to last st, k1.

Row 23: *K1, dyo; rep from * to last st, k1.
Rows 24–27: K1inc1, k1inc1, k to last st, k1inc1—66 sts.
Row 28: *K1, yo; rep from * to last st, k1.
Row 29: *K1, dyo; rep from * to last st, k1.
Rows 30–34: K1inc1, k1inc1, k to last st, k1inc1—81 sts.

BO sts loosely. Cut yarn and weave in ends.

FRINGES
Make 2 as foll:
Cut twenty 10"/25cm lengths of A
Cut ten 10"/25cm lengths of B
Use 10 strands of A and 5 strands of B for each fringe. Follow directions on page 19, Making Fringe, to create one fringe for each end of the scarf.

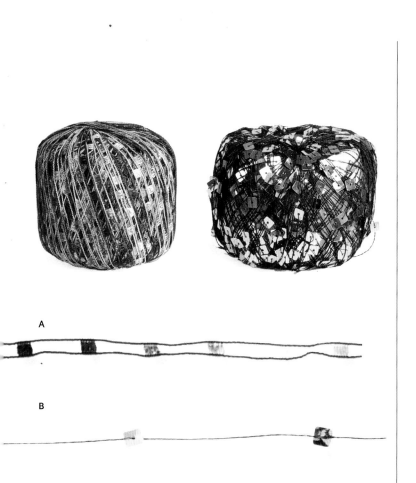

A

B

THIS PROJECT WAS KNIT WITH

A   2 balls of Trendsetter's *Binario*, 100% poly-
     ester, 0.9oz/25g, approx 82yd/75m per
     ball, color #107 Spices

B   2 balls of Berroco's *Mirror FX*, 100% poly-
     ester, 0.35oz/10g, approx 60yd/55m per
     ball, color Gold/Black #9003

ALTERNATE
This photo shows the project knit with Great
Adirondack's *Holographic Sequins*, 90%
rayon/10% polyester, color Grenada, and
Plymouth *Eros*, 100% nylon, color #3266.

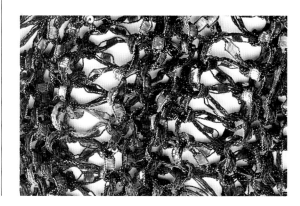

Glittering Eyeglasses Case

DESIGN BY
IRIS SCHREIER

SKILL LEVEL
◆ ◆ ◆ ◆
Intermediate

So elegant and stylish, this small case can hold glasses, or perhaps you can carry it as a clutch-style purse with an evening gown. It's a perfect gift, but be sure to purchase enough yarn, because you'll certainly want one for yourself as well.

Finished Measurements
6½ x 2¾"/17 x 7cm

Materials
Approx 100yd/91m variegated
fine weight sequin yarn in amethyst
Knitting needles: 2.75mm (size 2 U.S.) bamboo
needles *or size to obtain gauge*
Tapestry needle for sewing seams
Pins for fastening seams
¼"/1.6cm crystal bead or button
Sewing needle and thread for sewing bead or button

Gauge
31 sts and 64 rows = 4"/10cm in Garter Stitch
Always take time to check your gauge.

Instructions
Body
CO 50 sts.
K each row until piece measures 5½"/14cm from
bottom to top.

Flap
Begin dec for flap as foll:
Row 1: K2tog, k to last 2 sts, k2tog.
Rep row 1 (dec at the beg and end of each row)
until 10 sts rem.

Create buttonhole for flap as foll:
Row 1: K2tog, k1, k2tog, yo, yo, k2tog, k1, k2tog.
Row 2: K2tog, k1, k into front of 1st yo st, k1
into back of 2nd yo st, k1, k2tog—6 sts.
Row 3: K2tog, k2, k2tog—4 sts.
Row 4: K2tog, k2tog—2 sts.
BO rem 2 sts. Cut yarn and weave in ends.

Cut approx 24"/60cm of yarn and thread on tapestry needle. Put RS tog and pin seams. Sew edges
tog. Rep on other side. Turn RS out. Fold lower
flap so that it overlaps body of case by 2¼"/6cm.
Sew crystal bead or button into position so that
the buttonhole will fit snugly over it.

This project was knit with
1 hank of Great Adirondack's *Holographic Sequins,*
90% rayon/10% polyester, approx 100yd/92m,
color Amethyst

Knitting Abbreviations

beg *beginning*

beg pat *beginning of pattern*

BO *bind off*

CO *cast on*

cont *continue, continuing*

dec *decrease*

dpn *double-pointed needle(s)*

dyo *drop wrap, or yarnover, that was added in previous row*

foll *follow(s), following*

inc *increase*

k *knit*

k1inc1 *knit into front and back of same stitch, making two stitches out of one stitch*

k2tog *knit two stitches together, making one stitch out of two stitches*

p *purl*

p1inc1 *purl into front and back of same stitch, making two stitches out of one stitch*

p2tog *purl two stitches together, making one stitch out of two stitches*

pat *pattern*

pm *place stitch marker*

rem *remain, remaining*

rep *repeat*

RS *right side*

s1 *slip one stitch knitwise if following stitch is knit stitch, or purlwise if following stitch is purl stitch*

skkp *slip one stitch knitwise, knit two stitches, pass slipped stitch over both knit stitches (decrease from three stitches to two stitches)*

skp *slip one stitch knitwise, knit one stitch, pass slipped stitch over knit stitch (decreases from two stitches to one stitch)*

ssk *slip one stitch knitwise, slip another stitch knitwise, knit through both slipped stitches (decreases from two stitches to one stitch)*

spp *slip one stitch purlwise, purl one stitch, pass slipped stitch over purl stitch (decreases from two stitches to one stitch)*

sppp *slip one stitch purlwise, purl two stitches, pass slipped stitch over both purl stitches (decreases from three stitches to two stitches)*

st *stitch*

sts *stitches*

tog *together*

WS *wrong side*

yo *wrap yarn over needle, making an extra stitch, or yarnover*

Glossary

Drape—*The movement of a fabric; how it falls*

Elasticity—*The amount of springiness in a fiber; also known as give*

Fiber type—*The origin of the yarn, whether it comes from animal, plant, or synthetic (man-made) material*

Give—*The tendency of fabric to return to its original shape after it has been stretched; also known as elasticity*

Hand—*A combination of tactile qualities, including texture, durability, and fineness.*

Knitwise—*Pointing the needle into the stitch as if you are going to knit it.*

Loft—*Fluffiness of yarn.*

Purlwise—*Pointing the needle into the stitch as if you're going to purl it*

Texture—*The feel of the surface of the fabric, ranging from smooth to coarse.*

Acknowledgments

Our special thanks go to our editor, Suzanne Tourtillott, for becoming a knitter and catching our fervor in mind, word, and hand. Her guidance throughout the project and her uncanny ability to interpret our thoughts and words into beautiful language were indispensable, and we are most fortunate to have been given the opportunity to work with her.

To Carol Taylor and Nicole Tuggle at Lark Books, who immediately understood our design sense and were willing to take a chance with two relatively unknown fiber artists, our sincere thanks. Thanks also to Lark's indispensable Nathalie Mornu, who kept the details untangled. Thank you to Sandra Stanbaugh for your sharp eyes and ability to create such an exciting feast through your camera's lens. Our gratitude goes out to art directors Dana Irwin of Lark Books and Tom Petrucelli and Jim Bixby of 828 Inc., for so beautifully interpreting our sense of style directly onto the layout and pages of this book.

Very special love and thanks to the following family members who made a special contribution: Ruth, who helped knit many of the samples; Rita, who was always there for us with great feedback from Doug; Elliot, Ely, Einat, Eden, Alissa, and Owen, for helping with initial modeling and photography of the projects; Susan, for coming up with the idea for a sequined eyeglasses case; and Fred, for pointing us to Lark. Rebecca added a teenager's eyes and acumen to our designs and served as our consummate critic on color and style; she was also a most willing model. Thanks especially to Debby, for exemplifying a lifelong devotion to crafts.

In addition we'd like to thank the following friends and mentors: Cynthia, who constantly challenged us to come up with new luxury accessory ideas, some of which are included in this book; Claire, our fiber maven and mentor, who was always available for our questions; Nancy, whose color and design sense was invaluable; along with Elka and her mom, Sherry, our ever-knowledgeable technical expert and best knitting friend.

Last but not least, our love and thanks to our husbands and children, who put up with our incessant chatter, phone calls, and meetings, and who cooked and ran errands to give us more time to knit and write. We thank them for their encouragement and patience beyond the call of duty.

We'd also like to thank those fiber professionals who made suggestions and provided us with samples and their expertise:

Valerie at Knit'n'Tyme

Margery Winter at Berrocco

Jane and Kathy at Classic Elite

Susan at Crystal Palace

Samira and Ursula at Galler Yarns and Henry's Attic

Chuck at Jaggerspun

Diana at Mountain Colors

Kirstin at Muench

Yvonne at Plymouth

Fernando at Jacques Cartier Clothier, Inc.

Karen Selk at Treenway

Flora at Distinctive Yarns

David Blumenthal and Nancy Thomas at Lion Brand

And the additional companies that so generously provided us with yarns to sample, handle, and covet:

Anny Blatt

Blue Heron

Blue Sky Alpacas

Brown Sheep

Cascade Yarns

Dale of Norway

Fiesta Yarns

Great Adirondack

Habu Textiles

Harrisville Designs

JCA/Artful Yarns

Karabella

Kertzer

KFI

Knit One, Crochet Two

Lorna's Laces

Prism

Silk City

Skacel

Southwest Trading

Stacey Charles/Tahki

Swedish Yarn Import

Tess

Trendsetter

Westminster Fibers

About the Authors

Laurie Kimmelstiel draws much of the inspiration for her exotic designs from the varied ethnic makeup of her surroundings while growing up in the heart of New York City. She received an MA in American history from the University of Wisconsin and as a historian has noted a strong connection between craft and American social history. A knitter for many years, Laurie has taught the fiber arts to both young and old alike. She receives special pleasure introducing people to the joy and relaxation found in producing beautiful and exciting hand-knitted accessories. Her designs reflect a love of color and fiber as she explores the unusual and unpredictable in her creations. Handweaving is her other passion, and Laurie's work has been featured in *Handwoven* and *Ornament* magazines. She and her husband, a potter and surgeon, often exhibit their crafts together and display them on their website www.whiteridgecrafts.com. They live with their three children in an old house filled with pottery and yarn.

Iris Schreier comes from a long line of fiber artisans; one grandmother was a well-known European couturière and another the owner of a yarn shop. Her mother taught Iris to knit at a young age, and she later started designing accessories for herself and for friends. Her time spent working in the Soho district of New York City exposed her to fresh and hip urban street fashions that have inspired the accessories for this book. Iris's current passion is modular knitting, and she enjoys designing and uncovering new techniques that simplify the process. She writes a popular electronic newsletter on unique knitting techniques and designs, and publishes patterns that are sold at yarn shops through the world. She is in the process of authoring a new book for Lark Books on modular knitting techniques. Her art is displayed on her website, www.artyarns.com.

Index

Abbreviations, *139*

Acknowledgments, *141–142*

Angora, *12*

Bags, *90, 105, 108, 137*

Balaclava, *56*

Basics, *8–23*

Beads, attaching to tassels, *21*

Belts, *86, 88*

Belt ring, casting on and binding off, *22–23*

Boas. *See* Neckwear

Caps. *See* Headwear

Cases. *See* Bags

Cashmere, *12, 25*

Cast on, knitted, *22*

Circular needles, *14–16*

Cloches. *See* Headwear

Collars. *See* Neckwear

Color, *11*

Double knitting, *18–19*

Drape, *10*

Dye lots, *11*

Elasticity, *9–10*

Fiber types, *11–13*

Fringe, making, *19*

Gauntlets, *36*

Give, *9–10*

Glossary, *140*

Hand, *10–11*

Hats. *See* Headwear

Headwear, *32, 74, 96, 102, 114, 123*

Knitted cast on, *22*

Loft, *12*

Luster, *10*

Markers, placing on double-pointed needles, *18*

Merino, *11*

Modifying patterns, *13*

Mohair, *12*

Mufflers. *See* Neckwear

Neckwear, *26, 28, 30, 40, 42, 44, 50, 52, 54, 60, 62, 70, 73, 80, 94, 98, 116, 118, 120, 126, 128, 132, 134*

Needles, *9, 10, 11, 12, 14–16*

Point protectors, *16*

Purses. *See* Bags

Qiviut, *12, 25*

Rayon, *12*

Ribbon, *9, 10, 11*

Ribbon wrapping, *21*

Scarves. *See* Neckwear

Sequins, attaching to tassels, *21*

Shawls, *34, 44, 46, 64, 66, 78, 80, 98*

Silk, *12*

Stoles. *See* Shawls

Storing needles, *16*

Swatches, *13*

Synthetic fibers, *12*

Tassels, making, *20–21*

Techniques:

    beads, attaching to tassels, *21;*

    double knitting, *18–19;*

    fringe, making, *19;*

    markers, placing on double-pointed needles, *18;*

    ribbon wrapping, *21;*

    sequins, attaching to tassels, *21;*

    tassels, making, *20–21;*

    transferring to double-pointed needles from circular needles, *18*

Texture, *11, 12*

Tools, *14–17*

Transferring to double-pointed needles from circular needles, *18*

Weight, *9*

Wraps. *See* Shawls